How To Manage P
The No Waffle Guide To Managing Perfc
In The Workpl

Copyright © 2014 by Louise Palmer.

All rights reserved. No part of this publication may be reproduced, distributed, or transmitted in any form or by any means, including photocopying, recording, or other electronic or mechanical methods, without the prior written permission of the publisher, except in the case of brief quotations embodied in critical reviews and certain other non-commercial uses permitted by copyright law.

Table of Contents

Effective Managers 7
    Different Management Styles 7
    Situational Management 8
    Attributes of Successful Managers 10
    Management and Emotional Intelligence 12
Managing Teams 18
    Team Personalities 18
    Belbin Team Roles 22
    Emotional Intelligence in Teams 23
    Team Working Behaviours 27
Providing Feedback 29
    Feelings of Feedback 29
    Task Related Feedback 30
    Timing Issues 32
    Feedback Conversations 33
    Feedback That Leads To Higher Goals 35
Rewards 36
    Understanding Classical Conditioning 36
    Types of Reward 38
    Individual Targets 40
    Teamwork with Team Targets 41
    Teamwork with Individual Targets 41
Coaching 43
    The Difference Between Mentoring and Coaching 43
    When to use Coaching 44

- Benefits of Coaching 44
- Effectiveness of Coaching 45
- Underlying Psychology 46
  - Action Learning 46
  - GROW Model of Coaching 46
  - Inner Game 47
- Coaching Techniques 48
  - Setting Objectives 49
  - The Power of 'What' Questioning.......................................49
  - Avoiding 'Why' Questioning 50
  - Questions that Dig a Little Deeper 52
  - Using a Third Person 54
  - Using Scales...55
  - Maintaining A Positive Focus 55
  - Summarising and Providing Feedback 58
  - Looking for Patterns..59
  - Transferring what is working elsewhere. 60
- Reading the Coachee 61
- Different Levels of Listening 62
- Ethical Issues in Coaching 63
- In Summary 64

Understanding Stress 65
- What is Stress?..65
- The Word 'Stress' 67
- Perceptions of Stress 67
- The Costs of Organisational Stress..69

Causes of Stress at Work 70
    Factors Intrinsic To The Job 72
    Role In The Organisation 74
    Personality and Coping 75
    Relationships At Work 77
    Career Development 79
    Organisational Culture and Climate 80
    Home and Work Conflicts 80
Managing Stress 82
    Problem Solving Framework 82
Change Management 91
    Types of Change 91
    Five Laws of Organisation Development 91
    Transition Management Process – Involving the Employees 92
    Resistance to Change 93
    ADKAR 94
    Emotions to Expect During Change Programmes 96
    The Three Phase Process of Change 99
        Letting Go 99
        Neutral Zone 102
        New Beginning 105
    Why Transformation Efforts Fail 105
Appreciative Inquiry Method for Change Programmes 109
    The Positive Principle 110
    Appreciative Inquiry Critics 111
    5D Appreciative Inquiry Model 113

Appreciative Inquiry in Practice 115

References 122

Effective Managers

Different Management Styles

Managers can be task-orientated and/or person-orientated. Task-orientated managers focus on managing and completing the tasks that are assigned to the team. Person-orientated managers focus on managing the people who carry out the work. Whilst it depends on the environment as to which approach is best, in general, there usually needs to be a focus on both.

There are different management styles including transactional, transformational and laissez-faire.

Transactional Management Style

A manager who uses a transactional style sets goals for the team. If these goals are achieved, they receive rewards. These are considered 'transactions'. Managers tend to leave the team to complete their tasks and only get involved in there appears to be a problem. A transactional manager will spend time ensuring these transactions are completed successfully rather than providing true leadership. Most leaders and managers will need to use transactional management to some extent.

Transformational

Transformational management is more inspirational. Managers encourage their team to become involved and share thoughts and ideas. Managers take the time to provide formal and informal recognition for achievements. This type of manager encourages their team to be creative. They articulate a vision of the future and act as a role model that people wish to recreate in themselves. This type of management naturally motivates people.

Laissez-faire

This type of manager avoids making decisions and does not actively manage their team. They prefer to leave their team to get on with their work, even if there is clearly a need for them to get involved. Laissez-faire managers may be lacking in confidence, wish to avoid confrontation or lack the managerial skills required.

In some situations a Laissez-Faire style of management can be appropriate. It can encourage individuals and teams to solve their own problems and promotes autonomy. However, if a laissez-faire manager fails to take control of their team when it is required, it can hinder the team's success.

Situational Management

Different workplace situations require different management styles. Effective managers recognise this and adapt their management style accordingly (Hershey and Blanchard 1969). Solely relying on one management style can lead to poorly performing teams.

Do you manage the individuals in your team differently? Does their level of confidence, ability to complete tasks and attitude towards the task affect how you subsequently manage them?

Telling/Directing

If an employee has low commitment, low competence, is unable, unwilling, or insecure and lacks confidence, you should take a telling/directing approach. There needs to be a high task focus and low relationship focus.

You can aim to provide clear information on what is expected of the employee both in terms of the job and their conduct. You may try to discover the reason for the lack of motivation and enquire whether the employee needs further training or support. If you focus too much on the relationship, the employee may become confused as the boundaries feel blurred and they may begin to believe they do not have to do all the tasks required of them. It is important you provide clear task based instructions in this situation.

Selling/Coaching

When the employee has a degree of competence and perhaps is over-confident about their abilities, instructing them as to what to do, can reduce their motivation or lead to resistance.

You need to portray another way of working and sell its advantages. You need to create conversations around the tasks ensuring they actively listen. You may decide to use coaching to help this development process.

Participating/Support

When the employee is competent of the tasks required, yet is failing to complete them in a timely manner, you need to understand why. Once you know the reasons, you can try to address these to encourage the employee to complete the tasks as expected.

Employees cannot use their lack of ability as an excuse and you need to focus on motivation issues. It can help to praise the individual when they achieve the tasks required of them.

Delegating/Observing

When the employee is both competent and motivated, you can leave them to autonomously achieve the task. It is important that you still occasionally check their work to ensure they are maintaining their usual high standards.

An employee who is willing and able to complete their tasks with little intervention will need far less managerial input. However, it is important not to ignore the efforts and successes of these individuals as this could eventually lead to a lack of motivation. Regularly provide praise to ensure they feel valued and appreciated.

Attributes of Successful Managers

Research shows the following aspects contribute to long lasting success in high level executives (Eichinger and Lombardo 2004):

1. Intelligence
2. Technical/Operational Ability
3. Motivation
4. Experience
5. People Skills
6. Learning Abilities

1. Intelligence

In lower level roles, intelligence can impact on whether an employee is a poor or high performer. In senior level roles most executives have an adequate level of IQ. They have needed to demonstrate their intelligence in order to attain their current job role and therefore intelligence is not likely to predict whether a manager will be a poor or high performer.

A previously successful manager may start to struggle in a more senior role if they are unable to demonstrate Emotional Intelligence. Emotional Intelligence refers to how good they are with people.

2. Technical/Operational Ability

Technical and operational competence includes the executive's technical knowledge and ability to complete tasks successfully. It is not usually a large differentiator in the higher level jobs. This is because, like IQ, they have had to demonstrate a certain level of competence in order to achieve their current position.

3. Motivation

Usually those in senior manager roles have high levels of ambition. This ambition has provided them with the motivation to achieve their current position. As most high level managers possess high levels of motivation, it is not a differentiator between successful and non successful executives.

Intelligence, Technical/Operational ability and Motivation levels often impact on performance and differentiate workers in lower level positions. The levels of these elements are usually high in executives and are therefore not a differentiating predictor over which executives will enjoy long term success.

4. Experience

The types of experience a manager has had may impact on whether or not they are successful. These experiences might include previous management experience, their experience of being managed, seeing a project through from beginning to end, events of success, events of failure, problem solving and learning opportunities.

5. People Skills

The manager's ability to manage their own emotions, as well as other's emotions, is a predictor of management success. Lombardo and Eichinger (2003) state that people skills account for 6 out of the top 10 reasons for derailment. These include over managing, insensitivity, defensiveness, arrogance, the failure to build teams, and lack of composure. . It is important that a manager is able to manage their own emotions and the emotions of others. This is referred to as Emotional Intelligence (Goleman 1999). We will look at Emotional Intelligent management qualities shortly.

6. Learning Abilities

A key factor for management success is learning agility. Executives who derail view their learning to be complete. Whereas successful executives differ in that they tend to view learning as a continuous process. They are continually looking for new methods, better ways of working, alternative ways to think and they experiment with fresh approaches to old tasks.

Successful executives are motivated by their desire to educate themselves which enables them to make informed decisions and take considered risks. If they are faced with a problem which they do not have the knowledge or skills to solve, they conduct research and experiment with possible solutions until they achieve success. Learning agility is a large contributing factor to whether or not a manager will be successful.

Management and Emotional Intelligence

As already stated Emotional Intelligence (Goleman 1998) is a very important aspect of management success. Emotional Intelligence consists of a number of competencies. These include personal competencies and social competencies. Personal competencies relate to your ability to manage your own emotions. Social competencies relate to your ability to manage emotions in others.

The table below demonstrates the separate elements of Personal Competencies and Social Competencies.

Personal Competencies	Social Competencies
Self Awareness: Understanding the self.	**Social Awareness:** Awareness of other people's emotions, needs and anxieties.
Self Management: Management of emotions and desires. Emotional capabilities that aid goal achievement.	**Relationship Management:** Ability to evoke desired responses from other people.

Those managers who demonstrate high levels of emotional intelligence consistently outperform managers with lower levels of emotional intelligence. The competencies of a highly emotionally intelligent manager are listed below. As you read each competency, consider whether it highlights any development areas for you and whether you would like to address these.

PERSONAL COMPETENCE

SELF-AWARENESS

Emotional self-awareness. Managers high in emotional self-awareness are aware of their feelings and how they impact on others and their job performance. They are aware of their values and how these influence their actions. They are able to see the whole picture. They embrace both negative and positive feelings. They feel motivated and driven to achieve their goals.

Accurate self-assessment. Managers with high self-awareness know their strengths and limitations. They work to continually identify development areas and are open to receiving constructive feedback. They are comfortable enough to laugh at themselves. They are at ease asking for help and aware of what they need to do to further improve their performance.

Self-confidence. Managers high in self-confidence are able to accurately assess their strengths and abilities. They exhibit confidence with challenging tasks and projects. They display self-assurance.

PERSONAL COMPETENCE

SELF-MANAGEMENT

Self-control. Managers with the ability to demonstrate self-control are in command of their negative emotions. They channel them into positive outcomes. A manager with self-control stays calm during a crisis or if under stress. They remain calm and collected whatever the situation.

Transparency. Managers who demonstrate transparency talk freely with others regarding their emotions, thoughts, beliefs, values and actions. They are honest about their mistakes or faults. If they disapprove of another individual's actions, they will take considered action.

Adaptability. Managers with high adaptability are comfortable with constant change. They are able to work with multiple demands and keep their focus and energy throughout. They are comfortable with new ways of working.

Achievement. Managers who demonstrate high achievement levels set challenging, yet realistic, goals for themselves and their teams. They have a strong motivation and drive to achieve these goals. They encourage others who are lacking motivation. They ensure work is of a high standard. They evaluate risk accurately. They are driven to learn and encourage others to do the same.

Initiative. A manager high in initiative creates and seeks opportunities rather than waiting for them to present themselves as a result of circumstance. They strive to achieve positive change for the future.

Optimism. Managers high in optimism will look for opportunities in setbacks. They view others in a positive light and expect people to do their best. They are driven to create a positive working environment. They expect a positive future and work to make it a reality.

SOCIAL COMPETENCE

SOCIAL AWARENESS

Empathy. Managers who demonstrate empathy are able to read emotions in others and react appropriately. They ensure they actively listen to individuals, taking time to fully comprehend the other person's perspective. Their empathy makes it easy for them to build relationships with others from diverse backgrounds and cultures.

Organizational awareness. A manager with organizational awareness is able to look beyond formal job titles and analyse who really holds the most power. They understand crucial social networks and political aspects. They are aware of written and non-written rules that exist within the organisation.

Service. Managers high in the service competence regularly evaluate client satisfaction to ensure they are delivering the best service possible and meeting the client's needs. They encourage and foster an emotional climate to encourage positive interactions and relationships with clients.

SOCIAL COMPETENCE

RELATIONSHIP MANAGEMENT

Inspiration. Managers who inspire can liaise with others to develop a joint vision of the ideal future. They ensure that individual and team goals link to the overall goals of the organisation. They only ask others to do tasks that they would do themselves. They are passionate about the vision they create which encourages others to go beyond their required tasks in order to achieve the vision.

Influence. Managers who are successful at influencing others are persuasive and engaging. They understand how to influence people on an individual basis and this helps them to get buy in from key people.

Developing others. Managers who are effective at developing others feel motivated to help individuals achieve their full potential. They take into account the individual's capabilities and development areas. They take the time to provide regular positive and constructive feedback. They act as coaches and mentors to help individuals and teams reach their full potential.

Change catalyst. Managers who can act as change catalysts identify the need for change. They are able to communicate this need to others and gain support for the changes. They are able to maintain motivation during the change period and overcome any resistance.

Conflict management. Managers who are able to manage conflicts successfully ensure they take the time to listen to both parties' perspectives and fully understand the situation. They facilitate discussions between the parties and encourage them to keep statements task focused. They encourage the parties to work together to discover possible solutions to the task based conflict.

Teamwork and collaboration. Managers who are good team players are helpful and co-operative. They provide appropriate support and ensure they are involved with the tasks. They create a collective atmosphere as the whole team works towards the same goals and vision. They are able to develop close relationships with their team members that often go beyond work obligations.

You should by now have a good picture of what makes a successful manager. Let's contrast this to flaws that can derail managers. Zenger and Folkman (2009) conducted a management study using 360 degree surveys on 450, Fortune 500 executives. They then analysed the 11 000 least effective managers. They found these ineffective managers all had one or more of the following shortcomings:

- Lack of motivation
- Satisfied with their own average performance
- Did not hold a clear vision of the desired future
- Demonstrated poor judgements
- Were not keen to collaborate with others
- Did not act as a positive role model for others to follow
- Resisted change and new ideas
- Unable to amend behaviour after negative outcomes
- Low interpersonal skill level
- Did not further develop other people's skills

Interestingly the ineffective managers were unaware they exhibited these behaviours. Those who were rated the most negatively, rated themselves substantially more positively than the ratings they received. This demonstrates how important it is for managers to actively seek feedback from others.

Look back through the book so far and see if you can identify any areas that you think you could improve as a manager.

Create a list of action points you would like to address. Consider how you can improve your skills. You might choose workshops, online training courses, books, or internet research.

Managing Teams

When leading teams it is useful to identify the different personalities and working preferences of your team members. There are various tools we can use to help us identify the various aspects of a team.

Team Personalities

You may have heard of the Myers Briggs Type Indicator (MBTI). It is a tool which is used to assess different personality types. It highlights people's different psychological preferences and their perceptions of the world. It also identifies how people prefer to make decisions.

Below is a brief summary of the different personality types.

Introversion and Extraversion

People either lean towards introversion or extraversion when they make decisions.

Introversion
Thinks things through to reach a conclusion
Contemplates
Believes and understands
Thinks first, acts later
Seeks privacy
Concentrates on thoughts

Extraversion
Talks things through to reach a conclusion
Does
Shows
Acts first, thinks later
Seeks interaction
Thinks 'out loud'

Sensing and iNtuition

People are either sensing or intuitive in style when they consider information.

Sensing
Looks for facts
Acquires details first, then works out bigger picture
Enjoys present
Tends towards realism
Uses what's there
Uses trusted solutions
What is real

iNtuition
Looks for possibilities
Acquires overview first then looks at possibilities
Looks forward to the future
Tends towards idealism
Changes what's there
Creates own solutions
What might be

Thinking and Feeling

People are either thinking or feeling in how they make decisions.

Thinking
Decides using impersonal logic
True v False
Right v Wrong
Detached objectivity
Logical analysis and criticism
Organises
Detached

Feeling
Decides using subjective values
Likes v Dislikes
Good v Bad
Personal involvement
Sympathy and appreciation
Involved

Judging and Perceiving

People are either judging or perceptive in how they like to make final decisions and conduct the necessary activities.

Judging
Makes decision
Seeks closure
Plans and controls life
Structures
Prefers time to spare
Prefers things to be settled
Does task in hand

Perceiving
Acquires information
Maintains openness
Goes with the flow
Meanders
Last minute
Prefers change
Likes to explore all the opportunities the task presents

Go back through the MBTI psychological preferences and make a note of which describes you best:

Introversion or Extraversion?
Sensing or iNtuition?

Thinking or Feeling?
Judging or Perceiving?

Then take the first letter of each and you will have a four letter MBTI type. Note that for iNtuition, you would use the letter N. (This is just to introduce you to the concept and in no way replaces having your MBTI done professionally.)

Next, do this for a few members of your team.

What would likely happen if you were to have two opposites within your team, such as an ESTJ and an INFP?

How could knowing this help you to work more efficiently with your team?

Comment

If you had one team member that was an ESTJ and another team member who was an INFP, they may experience frustration with each other. The ESTJ type would likely want final decisions made and plans created. The INFP would prefer things to be more flexible and undecided. There are many different conflicts these two personality types could experience.

Work tasks can be designed to take into consideration people's differing personality traits. In addition, the understanding that friction is arising from these differences can in itself result in improved team cohesion.

MBTI and Problem Solving in Teams

When teams are working to solve problems, you can ask questions which appeal to either Sensing or Intuitive personality types.

Sensing: Ask questions about what is actually happening or has happened.
What are the facts?
What is the situation as it stands?
What has been tried before?
What has worked?

What has not worked?
What are the bottom line realities?
What resources do we have available?

Intuitive: Ask questions to discover prospects and potential possibilities.
What could we achieve?
What options do we have?
Can we look at this from another perspective?
What do the facts imply?
Does this issue relate to other issues we are experiencing?
Are there any patterns emerging?

When problem solving in teams, you can also satisfy both the Thinking and the Feeling personality types.

Thinking: Ask questions which evaluate each option.
What are the pros and cons of each option?
Are these options realistic?
Is there a risk to us if we do not act?
How do the options relate to our priorities?

Feeling: Ask questions which evaluate the emotive impact.
Is it in line with our values?
What impact will it have on the team?
What impact will it have on our customers?
Will it impact on work/life balance?
Will people need additional support?

Belbin Team Roles

Another useful tool for managing teams is Belbin's Team Roles. This tool helps you to understand the role each person naturally plays within your team. A team may not be effective because there is a vacant position that nobody naturally takes. This vacant role needs to be assigned to a team member/s. The roles include Plant, Resource-investigator, Co-ordinator,

Shaper, Monitor-evaluator, Team worker, Implementer, Completer Finisher, Specialist.

The table below details each of these roles.

Team Role	Contribution
Plant	Creative, imaginative, innovative.
Resource Investigator	Explores different opportunities, networks with external contacts and conducts research.
Co-ordinator	Formalises goals, encourages final decisions, encourages everyone's involvement.
Shaper	Works hard to overcome obstacles.
Monitor, evaluator	Considers all possible options, effectively evaluates.
Team Worker	Astute, insightful, diplomatic, emotionally supportive.
Implementer	Practical, task focused, considers finer details.
Completer Finisher	Ensures tasks completed in timely manner, develops in-depth plans for group tasks
Specialist	Provides specialist knowledge and skills.

Consider which roles your team members take. Are there any roles that are not currently filled by a team member? If so, does this role need to be allocated to a particular person?

Emotional Intelligence in Teams

eams which demonstrate high levels of Emotional Intelligence outperform teams with lower Emotional Intelligence (Goleman 1999). Highly emotionally intelligent teams are those where the individuals are good at managing their own emotions and others within the team. A highly emotionally intelligent team works cohesively and effectively. Research conducted by Druskat and Wolff (2001) identified norms that resulted in highly emotionally intelligent teams.

Norms – Individual Level

1. The team should be aware if a member is not on the same emotional wavelength. They need to acknowledge any negative statements. Doing so can make a person feel attended to and lessen the intensity of the negative emotion.

2. Time needs to be taken to consider different perspectives.

3. The team needs to consider each team member's thoughts on a task or situation. They need to specifically ask quiet members if they do not voluntarily contribute.

4. . If a concern is raised, it is important the team listens to the concern. The consequences of possible solutions should also be considered. Caution should be exercised when deciding a solution based on the majority vote.

5. Behaviour which crosses the line needs to be confronted. This can be achieved in a light-hearted manner.

Norms – Group Level

1. Teams need to self-evaluate their strengths and weaknesses. The team should celebrate goal achievement. They should actively encourage both positive and constructive feedback on work tasks in order to continually improve performance.

2. Team members should address any aspects of individual or team behaviour which may negatively affect team performance such as conflicts within the team. The effective team will then work to overcome this.

3. Teams need to favour optimism and focus on positive aspects rather than negative ones. Members need to be aware that their emotions, both

positive and negative, are contagious. Even in difficult situations, they need to consider what they can do with the resources available.

Norms - Emotions Outside the Group

1. The team needs to develop positive rapport and relationships with external teams. They may work to create opportunities for networking outside of the group.

2. The team needs to consider external team's needs, perceptions, thoughts and emotions. They can provide support to other teams and invite relevant individuals to attend team meetings.

3. Time should be taken to understand if the proposed actions are congruent with the organisations' culture and politics.

Use these Norms to answer the following questions.

Qu 1. A team have been informed that their head office have decided to integrate a new computer system. This means that all employees will need to attend a 5 day training course. One member of the team is clearly unhappy with the change. Make a note of what impact the following activities would have short and long term. Which option demonstrates the most emotional intelligence?

Option 1: Ignore their behaviour.
Option 2: Ask the team member what their concerns are.
Option 3: Ask the team member what their concerns are and work together to identify solutions.

Comment
Option 3 demonstrates the most emotional intelligence.

Qu 2. A member of the team is regularly taking an hour for lunch when only 30 minutes is permitted. Make a note of what impact the following activities would have short and long term. Which option demonstrates the most emotional intelligence?

Option 1: Joke about their lengthy lunch breaks in front of the team in the hope they will feel embarrassed and only take 30 minutes in future.
Option 2: Make no comment regarding their long lunch breaks.
Option 3: Take them to one side and ask what is making them take longer lunch breaks. Remind them that the rest of their team members are only taking 30 minutes and ask them to do the same.

Comment
Option 3 demonstrates the most emotional intelligence.

Qu 3. A team member has to change their normal shift in order to cover the absence of a colleague. They have had to cancel personal plans and arrive at the office in a clearly agitated state. Make a note of what impact the following activities would have short and long term. Which option demonstrates the most emotional intelligence?

Option 1: Apologise for the situation.
Option 2: When they arrive, publicly thank them for cancelling their plans and coming into the office at such short notice.
Option 3: Try to ignore their agitation.

Comment
demonstrates the most emotional intelligence.

Qu 4. A team have been working hard on a presentation for a client's project. The client did not like the ideas presented to them and is considering taking their custom elsewhere. The team usually enjoys positive feedback from clients and as a result of the meeting are feeling deflated and de-motivated. Make a note of what impact the following activities would have short and long term. Which option demonstrates the most emotional intelligence?

Option 1: The manager raises concerns over the quality of the team's ideas and presentation.
Option 2: The manager avoids talking about the situation with the team.
Option 3: The manager calls a meeting and reminds the team that he

believes them to be competent. He works with the team to consider possible solutions with the hope of trying to retain the client.

Comment
Option 3 demonstrates the most emotional intelligence..

Now look back over your notes regarding the impact of the different activities in the short and long term. What do you notice about the short and long term impact of **not** working in an emotionally intelligent way?

What do you notice about the short and long term impact of working in an emotionally intelligent way?

Comment
Some managerial actions may have little impact in the short term, however if repeated over time, they can have negative consequences for the team. Team cohesion can be affected.

A manager who continually demonstrates high levels of emotional intelligence, will ensure that his team works well together and performs to the best of their ability in both the short and long term.

Team Working Behaviours

Social Loafing

If a number of individuals work together as a team, there is a risk of 'Social Loafing'. Research has shown that as the number of people working on a task increases, the effort and/or performance from each person often reduce (Latane at al 1979).

This can be avoided if each person feels that their contribution can be identified and that their contribution makes a significant difference to the overall group achievement of the task (Kerr and Bruun 1983).

Groupthink

You will also need to be aware of group think. When working in groups the desire for unanimity and agreement takes over the clear evaluation of different options (Janis 1972). Other factors such as who holds power and self-esteem issues can also impact on group decisions.

It can be useful to review decisions in a few days time, to give individual members time to evaluate the different options on their own.

Providing Feedback

People rarely question positive feedback, yet they frequently question negative feedback (Snyder and Cowles 1979).

Negative feedback can at times be hard to come by (Audia and Locke 2003). If an individual is asked to provide feedback, they may feel comfortable providing positive feedback, yet shy away from providing negative feedback. As a manager it is important that you provide both positive and negative feedback to your team members, but it is a delicate process. You need to communicate that you still think the employee is competent, and you are happy with their performance overall. We often hear employees comment along the lines of, 'I am told in one breath that my work is good and then in the other that I have all these faults. Nothing I ever do is good enough.'

Feelings of Feedback

It can be difficult for an individual to listen to negative feedback. This remains true even if they have asked for your honest feedback on a particular task they have completed. When receiving feedback people may:

Blame others for their actions
Feel threatened
Take things personally
React defensively
Give the impression they are wishing to develop, when they have no intention to do so
Experience lower self esteem
Feel less confident
Feel deflated
Feel a lower sense of achievement
Feel anxious in anticipation of feedback
React positively and thrive on the feedback, using it for development

With these thoughts in mind, consider what might be on a 'Best Practice - Effective Feedback' handout sheet, in order to limit these negative effects.

Task Related Feedback

There are various techniques you can use to limit the negative feelings of developmental feedback. It is very important to ensure you focus on the task rather than the person. Be concrete and discuss specific examples to illustrate. For example rather than saying 'You are underperforming' you could say 'you missed your targets last week and again this week'.

If an individual is unable to complete a task to your satisfaction, you should consider whether the task is too difficult. It might need to be broken down into sections or require the involvement of additional team members. When designing or allocating work tasks, ensure they are within your employee's capabilities. Continually assigning difficult tasks, which the employee is unable to successfully complete, can cause lasting damage to their confidence levels.

However, it is also important that the employee experiences a degree of challenge from their work tasks. If you show your confidence in the individual's ability to complete the task, you will positively impact on their confidence levels.

When providing an employee with feedback, ensure the feedback relates to specific, task focused elements that the employee can actively improve upon. There is no point in criticising an individual for not being creative when they are not a naturally creative person.

Help them to develop to the best of their ability. During feedback sessions jointly look for solutions. Regularly check their progress.

This conversation between a trainer and delegate happened when discussing feedback during one of our public training courses:

Delegate: I used to be awful at receiving feedback. I think my managers sometimes held back their real thoughts on my work as they didn't want to face my negative reaction to their criticism. It would usually end in an argument. Once I had calmed down, I would see their point of view and usually agree. I would then work hard to address the negative feedback I had received. I feel these days I still react badly to negative feedback, but I think the intensity of my reaction has lessened. I try to remind myself that they are only trying to help me improve.

Trainer: What was it that used to make you angry?

Delegate: I don't really know. I think I felt hurt that my work was being criticised. I had worked so hard on it and then someone had just come along and ripped it apart. I took it personally.

Trainer: You say that you cope better with feedback now. What's changed?

Delegate: I changed jobs and started working with a new manager. I think he was surprised by my reaction the first few times he gave me negative feedback, particularly as I'm usually quite a reserved person. He reassured me, stating that he had given me the job because he knew I was competent and I had proven this to him in my work. He said that his negative feedback did not imply that he felt I was performing poorly. He simply wanted to discuss the tasks in question and how I could have managed them differently in order to achieve even better results. He made me realise that when anybody gives me feedback they are not questioning me in general, they are questioning my approach to that particular situation. I can now distance myself from the specific task. I still initially feel angry but I can now talk myself down.

In this situation, the manager explained the reasons behind his feedback and reassured the individual that they were performing well in their role. The manager was providing development guidance to the individual in relation to specific tasks rather than providing generalised, or personal, negative feedback. This helped the delegate change their perspective on receiving feedback.

Look back at the list you created for your handout on providing feedback. Did you have anything regarding timing? If not, consider if timing has an impact.

Consider your own experiences of receiving positive and negative feedback. Would you prefer to hear positive feedback, followed by negative feedback? Or negative feedback followed by positive feedback? Consider the impact each option had.

Timing Issues

In general terms it is advised to provide positive feedback first and then encourage the individual to identify possible development areas. Doing it in this order encourages commitment and further self-reflection. It could be argued that it would be better to provide the positive after the negative as the individual will then leave the session on a positive note. However, positive after negative can often be considered as insincere. The individual may believe they have just been told something positive to make them feel better. In a positive feedback situation the development areas and future goals should ensure the individual leaves feeling positively motivated.

Imagine that your employee just had a meeting with a client that resulted in a negative outcome. Do you think it would be better to meet immediately to discuss the situation and provide constructive feedback, or schedule a meeting for a later time/date? Again consider various scenarios.

Whilst in some situations it is appropriate to deal with the situation straight away, sometimes it can cause problems as emotions are still running high. It is usually best to schedule the discussion for later that day. This gives you time to calm down and the individual time to reflect before the meeting.

It is possible that the individual may subsequently worry about the meeting however, usually the meeting is more productive as both parties will be calmer and able to adopt a rational perspective.

Feedback Conversations

Feedback is often subjective. Your perspective on the situation may well differ to another manager's perspective. Therefore it is important that you present your feedback as your opinion, based on the facts and information you currently have.

Ensure that you are actively listening to the individual. They may have information that is currently unknown to you. In light of this information you might gain a different perspective on the incident.

Lizzio et al (2008) evaluated the effectiveness of negative feedback systems in the workplace. The research discovered the most effective approach was to:

1. Provide Negative Feedback

2. Immediately seek the individual's reflections/views on the feedback you have just provided.

Listen to the employee's perspective on the situation and ask questions if necessary. Make sure you fully understand their viewpoint.

Be respectful. If possible, acknowledge that you can see why the individual acted as they did. You might say 'I see why you chose that option however.....' or perhaps 'I can understand why you did xyz, however....' It provides them with reassurance that they approached the task competently, yet some development areas exist. Demonstrating that you believe them to be competent reduces negative reactions and is more likely to encourage them to embrace the development areas you suggest.

When providing constructive feedback, ensure you do not overwhelm the employee by suggesting too many development points. This could create defensiveness. People can only take in so much at a time. If possible try to pick a few key points to focus on.

When providing feedback to employees, ensure that you are not making generalisations, use specific examples. Avoid using all or nothing words like 'always' and 'never', as the recipient can probably remember exceptions. If they bring these up, it can weaken your position.

Avoid referring to third parties, for example, 'Mr X tells me you are micromanaging'. This will give the individual the impression that other colleagues are talking about them.

Avoid feedback that tries to analyse the reason behind the individual's behaviour, for example, 'I know that you are going through some difficult times at home'.

Ask employees to inform you of their achievements. This can be done in ad-hoc, informal manner whereby the employee informs you as and when they achieve a certain task or goal, or more formally during performance appraisals.

Although receiving constructive feedback can invoke negative emotions in employees, it is necessary in order to further develop employees. In fact, not receiving any feedback, positive or negative, from managers can cause employees to feel stressed and anxious. The uncertainty that a lack of feedback brings can be unsettling. An individual may be left trying to second guess their manager's thoughts. This is a comment from one of our delegates during a public training course:

"I really like to receive feedback. I like to learn how to improve myself. As work is so busy at the moment, I haven't had supervision for 3 months. I really miss it. My manager doesn't even make the odd comment regarding how well I'm doing, or not doing. I have no idea if they think my work is great or awful!"

Feedback That Leads To Higher Goals

Positive feedback not only builds natural strengths, it fosters positive emotion.

Locke and Latham (1990) have repeatedly shown that goal setting is effective in raising performance. Seo & Remus (2009) have developed this further. They discovered that people who experience positive emotion in their work, spend more time trying to achieve their goals. This results in higher levels of performance. Employees that receive positive feedback, enjoy higher levels of confidence which results in an increased likelihood of attempting more challenging tasks.

Managers need to ensure they provide plenty of positive feedback. They may believe that continually highlighting an employee's mistakes will improve the employee's performance. However, Seo suggests that if the continual feedback invokes negative emotion in the employee, they will feel criticised and are more likely to reduce their own expectations of what they can achieve. As a result, they will attempt less challenging goals in future.

Think of a feedback situation that is likely to happen in the future. Using the ideas in this book, design a plan for how you would carry out this feedback.

Rewards

Understanding Classical Conditioning

It is important to understand how rewards reinforce employee's behaviour.

Many of you will have heard of Pavlov and his dogs. Pavlov was originally studying the digestive and nervous system of dogs, which he won a Nobel Prize for in 1904. After the dogs were in the laboratory for a short while he noticed the dogs started to salivate upon seeing their food dish or even just hearing the feeder's footsteps.

This indicated some form of basic learning. Pavlov designed an experiment that measured the amount of saliva. He would ring a bell just before putting food into dogs' mouths. After repeating this several times, he discovered the sound of the bell alone caused the dogs to salivate.

The psychologist Skinner differentiates between two different types of behaviour:

Classical conditioning - a stimulus generates a natural response, as in Pavlov's experiment.

Operant behaviour - behaviours operate on the environment and are reinforced.

Human behaviour is mainly operant behaviour, for example learning a musical instrument, riding a bike or writing an effective report. Consider an employee who delivers an in house training course for other employees. During the training course they receive positive engagement from their colleagues which encourages them. After the training course they receive positive feedback forms. These are considered to be 'rewards'. The employee will likely replicate these thoughts and actions in future training courses as they result in rewards.

We sometimes reinforce behaviour without even knowing it. Positive reinforcement includes actions of attention, praise, recognition, material rewards, time, smiles, laughter etc. We also reinforce negative behaviour unwittingly by providing time and attention to people displaying negative behaviours.

Employees will receive many positive rewards in the workplace. These may include formal rewards such as bonuses, promotions or pay increases, or more subtle rewards of recognition and compliments. Their positive behaviour is rewarded. This positive reinforcement provides them with the drive and motivation to further develop their skills and achieve success.

Do you think managers should therefore provide positive reinforcement each time they notice an employee acting in a desirable way? What might the impact of this be?

Research has shown that continuous positive reinforcement can be detrimental to people as they can begin to rely on it. If they do not receive the reward as expected, it can de-motivate them. Positive reinforcement will create more of an impact if it used frequently but not continuously.

What factors might you take into consideration when praising an individual or team?

When praising an individual or team, select a specific aspect of their behaviour you would like to praise. It is important to praise everybody from time to time.

Most people like to receive praise and as a result employees may focus more on the work tasks which result in them receiving attention and compliments. This could result in them focusing less effort on the more necessary day-to-day tasks, such as administration or record keeping. These day-to-day tasks may be deemed as less important in the employees mind.

At times individuals might appear highly motivated however their work outputs are relatively low. This may be due to the fact that they are focusing on the elements of the role that receive the most positive reinforcement and are disregarding other important tasks.

Types of Reward

There are two types of rewards in the workplace, intrinsic and extrinsic.

Intrinsic refers to rewards that are gained from certain elements of the job. The employee may enjoy working on certain tasks and feel satisfied upon their successful completion. The tasks which invoke these intrinsic rewards are usually challenging, autonomous, make a difference to others, develop relationships or provide instant feedback. These intrinsic rewards are self-administered.

Extrinsic rewards are those that are received externally. These include pay, promotions, bonuses, recognition and personal development opportunities. These extrinsic rewards are administered by someone else.

Extrinsic reward systems motivate people to increase their performance and productivity. It should be noted that once the extrinsic reward is removed the motivation is likely to reduce (Pritchard et al 1976). Jobs which offer elements of intrinsic rewards, which are by their very nature naturally rewarding, often result in greater fulfilment.

Consider individuals on a bonus scheme (extrinsic reward). They achieve their targets and receive the bonus. How long does the motivation last for? Do you think it makes the employee feel happy at work in both the short and long term?

Bonus schemes can create happiness and satisfaction. However, these feelings are often short lived if the role does not also hold intrinsic rewards.

If a person receives solely extrinsic rewards from their role, it can result in decreased levels of satisfaction, dedication and commitment. It can also increase exhaustion and places them at higher risk of burn-out. After achieving a target, the individual might experience a period of elation, however this will often be short-lived. Research has shown that higher salaries have a limited ability to moderate these effects. People often feel tied to these jobs because of the extrinsic rewards yet feel a real desire to leave. This often results in the individual calculating what minimum effort is required in order to achieve these rewards.

The impact of these largely extrinsic reward roles can make an impact not only on the person's well-being in the workplace, but it can also filter in to their home lives. The employee may feel exhausted by the time they finish their workday and chose to do as little as possible in the evenings. They may stop spending quality time with families and friends as they simply don't have the energy. Impending work days can lead to feelings of depression and detachment.

If possible, a manager should try to ensure that there are opportunities for the employee to receive intrinsic rewards. This can be achieved by providing work tasks which are appropriately challenging, require creativity and allow for employee autonomy.

The next section of the book is going to look at the types of rewards that be given in the workplace. These include contrived on the job rewards and natural rewards.

Contrived On The Job Rewards:

Consumables - consumables refer to things that are consumed. For example, tea, coffee, other refreshments, chocolates, cakes, after work drinks.

Objects - desk accessories, nice stationary, company vehicles, watches, formal reward badges.

Visual & Auditory – pleasant working environment, natural light and working windows, small or private offices, ability to listen to music, guest presenters, regular feedback, coaching, mentoring.

Monetary – bonuses, shares, health insurance, entertainment tickets, holidays, day trips, shopping vouchers, profit sharing.

Natural Rewards:

Social – recognition, attention, lunch invites, requesting opinion or assistance, positive feedback, praise, requests for contributions on company blog.

Working Hours & Promotion – flexible working, unexpected time off work, promotion.

One of the most common rewards is monetary. Many companies use performance related pay schemes. What impact do you think Performance Related Pay has on an

- Individual?

- Team?

Individual Targets

Performance related pay schemes can motivate employees. They can give a person a sense of purpose and encourage them to strive to reach targets. Research shows that performance is increased when workplaces use performance related pay schemes. However, it should also be noted they can cause unwanted behaviours.

Some individuals on the schemes hold back on their performance. Imagine a lawyer who has been set a target by his manager to achieve £120k of chargeable fees in one year. They exceed their target by 10K and achieve £130k of fees. Due to this, next year their target rises to 140K. In order to achieve this target, the lawyer would have to work extremely hard.

Some employees, if set a target of £120k, would aim to achieve fees just over this target, for example £123k. This would mean that the target they are set for the following year is much more achievable. Their next year target might then only be £133k. They knowingly build in a bit of breathing space. So the company in this example would lose about £7k in fees. Hitting targets can act as a punishment as employees then have to work even harder next year. One way to combat this is to set different types of goals. Alternatively the bonus structure could be based on percentages, for example, once an individual has reached their initial target, offer a percentage of their additional fees as a bonus.

Another negative factor of performance related pay is that in order to hit the targets some individuals indulge in unwanted behaviours. Employees who have targets that are difficult to reach may act in a way that could be detrimental to the company. For example, they may mis-sell products or services, go against company policies and procedures, or inflate the length of time spent working on a client's project. These actions enable the employee to reach their targets with less effort. People may not take holidays or absence leave when sick as monthly targets often do not take this into account. High targets can result in burn-out as individuals have to work longer hours with less breaks in order to achieve them. It can often result in mistakes.

Teamwork with Team Targets

Teams with team targets can encourage every member of the team to work hard. It naturally promotes team work. However, it can also cause conflicts if some colleagues are deemed to be under-performing in comparison to the rest of the team.

Teamwork with Individual Targets

The impact of individual targets on team work can have positive and negative effects. It can lead to a highly motivated team who are all striving to achieve. However, team work can be hampered as individuals are concerned with achieving their own targets. Individuals may be reluctant to take time out of their day to help a colleague as it puts them behind and creates additional pressure.

In addition, in this economic climate some companies have found that they are unable to pay promised bonuses, which leads to negative feelings such as lack of trust and low motivation.

Think about what intrinsic and extrinsic rewards motivate you at work. To what extent do they motivate you? What motivates you the most? To what extent do you think the various rewards would motivate your individual team members? What would motivate them the most?

One thing to bear in mind is that people are motivated differently. One person might be motivated by money, others by status and others by making a difference (Francis 1994). There is a tool called the Career Drivers Survey which asks a number of questions to identify what motivates the individuals in your team. You can find this survey if you use an internet search engine and type in Career Driver Survey. It's free and a great tool. Once you have discovered what motivates your individual team members, you can design suitable rewards systems for your team. Reward systems should ideally consist of both extrinsic and intrinsic rewards. The extrinsic rewards will probably remain largely unchanged due to the monetary cost however you may be able to provide additional training to employees through in house training courses, mentoring or coaching. The intrinsic rewards you decide to incorporate can easily be introduced into everyday working life. They can provide positive reinforcement and increase employee satisfaction and motivation.

Coaching

Coaching is a process which aims to develop various aspects of an individual. Coaching can be used on a one-to-one basis, with a team, or a whole department. You can use coaching as a sit down exercise where you perhaps take an hour to deliver a coaching session, or you can use coaching questions in daily working life to continually develop your team. The person providing the coaching is referred to as the 'Coach' and the person receiving the coaching is the 'Coachee'.

The Difference Between Mentoring and Coaching

In order to fully understand the purpose of coaching, it is useful to compare it to mentoring. The mentoring process involves transferring the mentor's knowledge and expertise to another individual. The mentor provides detailed and specific instructions for the task. Many organisations use mentoring as a way to train their employees and also to keep knowledge within the company. Mentoring can lead to coaching.

A coach does not have to be an expert on the subject, whereas a mentor does. The coach uses a variety of methods such as asking specific timed questions. They aim to provide the individual with a greater awareness of their approach to the situation, assisting them to develop of their own solutions.

The key principles of coaching include:
- Working collaboratively with the coachee.
- Focusing on helping the coachee to achieve their coaching goals.
- Ensuring the focus remains solely on the coachee's thoughts and experiences.
- Encouraging the coachee to make changes by raising their awareness of their thought patterns and behaviours.

When to use Coaching

Coaching is most valuable when approaching a situation or challenge that has no one correct answer. If there is a correct answer, for example, in how to complete a specific task, then training or an instruction based approach is more appropriate.

Coaching empowers individuals to develop their own solutions. It achieves this through asking a series of questions and using reflection techniques.

Benefits of Coaching

There are many benefits to coaching:

Improved Performance and Productivity - Coaching encourages the individual to have a greater awareness of their own thoughts and behaviour. The individual being coached has time to reflect on how they are approaching work tasks and ultimately this leads to a more considered approach. This in turn leads to increased performance and productivity.

Improved Learning and Development - Coaching is used to enhance the coachee's performance in the workplace. It encourages learning and behaviour change over an extended period (Wasylyshyn et al 2006).

Improved Relationships - Coaching naturally builds rapport and improves relationships. Research shows that we like people who actively listen to us. As this is one of the main roles of the coaching session, the Coachee will naturally view the coach positively.

More Motivated Staff - Coaching improves motivation. In general, individuals like to feel they are progressing. They will enjoy a sense of achievement from achieving their goals.

Greater Flexibility and Adaptability to Change - Coaching encourages a flexible attitude towards change. Many coaches find they start to coach themselves and continue to use this life skill to manage future challenges.

Many people find that these skills also naturally filter into their personal lives.

Executive Coaching

Executive coaching refers to the coaching of managers and senior managers. Research indicates that executive coaching results in:

- Effective people management
- Improved interpersonal relationships
- Increased ability to prioritise goals
- Higher commitment to the task or role
- Increased performance and productivity
- Improved dialogue and clearer communication (Kombarakaren et al 2008)

Executive coaching is particularly beneficial if it is used in conjunction with formal leadership development training courses, performance appraisals and reward systems. Using this whole approach can result in a higher business impact (Levenson 2009).

Any coaching conducted in the workplace, regardless of the coachee's role, can also be linked to the organisation's mission statements and goals.

Effectiveness of Coaching

How successful a coaching session will be depends on a number of contributory factors. These include the coach's attributes (Kilburg 1996), the coachee's attributes (Kilburg 1997) and the working environment (Argyris 1994). It might be that the coach is fantastic and the coachee really wants to change but the working environment is limiting the success. Research shows the main factor affecting whether or not the coaching sessions will be successful is the extent to which the coachee wishes to change.

A coachee's readiness to change can also affect the degree to which the coaching sessions are successful. Sometimes it may not be the right time to be moving forward. It might be the coachee is lacking in confidence or perhaps they are experiencing a difficult time in their personal lives. Coaching can still be beneficial in this situation but would simply need to focus more on increasing confidence levels or increasing the individual's desire to change.

Underlying Psychology

Various psychological theories and models underpin the coaching process.

Action Learning

One of the underpinning theories of coaching is that of Action Learning. Action learning refers to learning through 'doing' rather than from being given instructions. Learning by 'doing' requires the individual to be willing to learn. They also need to be able to adopt a reflective attitude, and accept and process positive and constructive feedback. The individual should be keen to view situations or challenges as an opportunity to learn. Professor Reginald Revans is the originator of action learning. When working for the coal board, he sometimes encouraged managers to meet together in small groups to discuss experiences and share information in order to learn from each other. He realised that when he did so, productivity increased over 30%.

GROW Model of Coaching

There are various models of coaching. One of the most popular is the GROW model of coaching:

(Topic – initial understanding of the coaching task & setting the meta goal.)

Goal - The coach and coachee work together to create a set of objectives for the session.

Reality - An exploration between the coach and the coachee of exactly what they are trying to achieve. This includes questions around who, what, when, where and how.

Options - A consideration of what is actually possible and the pros and cons of each option.

Wrap-up - Involves a summary of the session's key action points and a discussion of potential obstacles (e.g. commitment, work environment). This carries forward to the next session.

In organisational settings the Topic is usually set by a senior manager, line manager or the coach. For example the line manager might say, 'I want person X to achieve Y'.

Inner Game

Inner Game theory demonstrates why the coaching process continually results in successful outcomes. The theory also underpins the GROW model of coaching.

Inner Game theory was developed by Timothy Gallwey. Gallwey was a tennis coach. He realised that when he pointed out mistakes to his tennis pupils, they initially amended their techniques yet the change was short-lived. Eventually they would revert to making the same mistakes. Gallwey realised the instructional process was not working and he needed an alternative approach. He asked his coachee to narrate their play. This naturally raised their awareness of their actions and kept their eye on the ball.

Gallwey asked his students what they felt was working and what wasn't. The students analysed their play and were able to identify what worked and what did not work. This provided them with their own instructions and resulted in them improving their techniques with a relatively small amount of effort. He termed this the 'Inner Game'.

Inner Game Theory demonstrates that people have the knowledge within themselves to develop their own solutions. Coaching brings this knowledge into consciousness and enables them to solve their own problems and achieve their goals.

If an individual has identified the solution themselves rather than receiving a set of instructions, they are far more likely to retain the learning points (Alexander, Fine & Whitmore 2002).

Coaching Techniques

There are a wide variety of coaching techniques that you can use. Some techniques will be used each session, whereas others will only be employed as and when they suit the situation. There are various skills you need when coaching people:

Ability to Building Rapport and Relationships - Whilst rapport is built naturally from the coaching session, the coach needs to have good interpersonal skills. It is important they show empathy and compassion to the coachee. They also need to provide encouragement at all times.

Ability to Ask Appropriate Questions – It can be tempting for a coach to ask questions for their own personal interest. However, the only questions which should be asked of the coachee are those will raise the coachee's self-awareness, help them to develop solutions and achieve their goals.

Ability to Actively Listen - The coach needs to actively listen to the coachee and not just remain silent. The coach also needs to ensure they allow a period of silence after the coachee has finished answering the question. This silence can allow the coachee to further reflect upon their answer and add to it if necessary.

Ability to Notice Subtle Changes in Others - It is important to look for changes in behaviour in order to monitor the well-being of the coachee.

Ability to Provide Useful Feedback – It is important the coach has the ability to provide both positive and constructive feedback.

Setting Objectives

First, the coach needs to find out what the coachee's goals are. When setting objectives during the coaching process you need to make sure they are specific, measurable, achievable, realistic and timed.

Specific
Measurable
Achievable
Realistic
Timed

The Power of 'What' Questioning

This next section looks at the 'what' questions you might want to use in a coaching session or when trying to develop your staff. The questions you choose will depend on what seems appropriate at the time. You might find you wish to change the wording slightly to make the question feel more natural to you.

Questions starting with the word 'What' help to:
Identify and investigate the problem in more depth.
Aid implementing the action plan.
Assist the decision making process.
Analyse how much power the individual has over the situation or outcome.
Increase motivation for the task.
Clarify the next steps of the action plan.

Questions to identify and investigate the problem in more depth:
What would you consider a successful outcome to be?
What is the minimum outcome that you would be happy with?
What is the ideal outcome?
What do you think caused that to happen?

Questions to assist with implementing the individual's plans:
What support are you going to need?
What order do you need to achieve these goals in?

Questions to assist the decision making process:
What are the possible options?
What are the pros and cons of each option?
What is most important to you?
What would have the biggest impact?

Questions to check how much power the coachee has over the outcome:
What other factors are at play?
To what extent do you have control over the outcomes?
What impact will other people have on the outcomes?
To what extent are you responsible for being successful?
What can you do to make sure you are successful?
What obstacles might occur and what can you do about these?

Questions to increase motivation for the task:
What impact would achieving this have on you?
What impact would not achieving this have on you?
What impact will achieving this have on future goals?
What would others think of you if you managed to achieve this?

Questions to clarify the next steps:
What are the steps you need to take in order to achieve your goal?
What is the first step/next step?
What do you need to do to prepare for the next step?

Avoiding 'Why' Questioning

'Why' questioning can often be seen as blaming or fault finding. In coaching sessions, it is best avoided if possible as it can make the coachee feel defensive.

So let's look at an example. Instead of 'Why did you not do the work that Bob asked you to complete?' try ' Was there a reason for the delay on Bob's work?'

This could then be followed by asking the coachee how they could manage the situation differently should it arise again.

Activity

Re-write the following sentences to avoid starting them with the word 'Why'.

Why are you continually late in submitting your end-of-month reports?
Why do you keep making these mistakes?
Why are we receiving complaints about you from the client?
Why are you not answering the client's calls?
Why are you letting the team down and not hitting your monthly targets?

Comment

Of course you may have different answers to the below, however, these examples will give you some ideas.

Why are you continually late in submitting your end-of-month reports?
What prevented you from finishing your end-of-month reports on time?

Why do you keep making these mistakes?
What is causing these mistakes?

Why do we keep receiving complaints about you from the client?
What is causing the client to make complaints about you?

Why is it taking you up to a week to return the client's telephone calls?
The client has said that you are taking up to a week to return their calls, what is causing this to happen?

Why are you letting the team down and not hitting your monthly targets?
Okay, so you are not hitting your targets. What is preventing you from doing so?

Questions that Dig a Little Deeper

You can ask the question 'what else?' in order to dig a little deeper. You can ask 'what else' once, or you can continue to repeat it. When we do this exercise in our public training courses, it often causes a lot of laughter as it really challenges the coachees' thinking. You can either use the 'What else' question or try 'what difference would that make?' Below are two real-life examples of this technique.

Transcript from a coaching session:
Coach: What would you like to achieve in your position in the next few years?
Coachee: I'd really like to be considered for a promotion.
Coach: What are the things that you need to do in order to be in this position?
Coachee: I probably need to work a bit harder, step up my game.
Coach: What would this entail?
Coachee: Maybe get in earlier in the mornings so that I have more time to do my work.
Coach: And what else?
Coachee: Maybe stay later.
Coach: And what else?
Coachee: Show my work to the senior management team so they know what I do.
Coach: And what else?
Coachee: Improve some of my skills, perhaps go on a few training courses to update my skills.
Coach: And what else?
Coachee: Get involved in out-of-work activities. I usually miss these as I can't be bothered but they might be a good opportunity to get to know the senior managers.
Coach: And what else?
Coachee: Ummmm....not sure...(coach remains silent).....ummm.....see if I get involved in some of the various committees or focus groups.
Coach: And what else?

Coachee: Errr......(coach remains silent)....see if I could contribute to the company's blog.

You can see in this scenario that the coachee starts to struggle. The coach just remains silent in order to give the coachee time to think. Using the 'what else' technique helps the coachee to think of various options rather than just the first one or two options that come to mind.

Here is an example of a transcript where the coach used the 'what difference would that make' technique.

Coach: What would like to change about yourself?
Coachee: I'd like to be more assertive at work.
Coach: What difference would that make?
Coachee: I would be able to put forward my ideas without worrying that people will think I am stupid.
Coach: What difference would that make?
Coachee: The senior managers would see that I have some good ideas that could make a real difference to the business.
Coach: What difference would that make?
Coachee: They would respect me more and I might be considered for a promotion.
Coach: What difference would that make?
Coachee: Well if I got a promotion, I would get more money and that would mean I was more financially secure.
Coach: What difference would that make?
Coachee: I wouldn't worry about money so much and would probably feel a lot less stressed, particularly when I have to pay for things like an MOT or insurance.
Coach: What difference would that make?
Coachee: I would be more relaxed.
Coach: What difference would that make?
Coachee: I would be able to enjoy my life more, my family would probably get more of the real me.

You can see how this scenario went from wishing to be more assertive to enjoying life more. It can be enlightening for the coachee to think through why they want things. This can really motivate a coachee.

Activity
Take some time to think of 5 of your own personal goals.
Try repeatedly asking yourself:
'What else? What else?'
'What difference would that make? What difference would that make?
Refer back to the previous two slides to get yourself started.

Using a Third Person

It can be useful to introduce a third person's perspective when the coachee:
- Is unable to think of possible solutions.
- Needs more options to choose from.
- Might find it helpful to consider the situation from a more senior person's perspective e.g. a CEO.
- Needs to visualise success in order to increase motivation.

As an example you could ask:
'How do you think the CEO would manage this?'
'What thoughts do you think the CEO would have if they were in this situation?'
'How do you think the CEO would have dealt with their feelings?'

In order to increase motivation you could ask:
'What would the CEO notice about you?'

If a coachee responds with an answer and you believe that the third person would not act in this way, do not try to correct them. Let them make their own conclusions.

Other example third person questions include:
'What would the CEO have noticed if you were confident?'
'What would the CEO have noticed that you were doing differently?'

'What would the CEO have noticed about your mood?'
'What would the person at the bus stop notice about your mood?'
'What would your friend do in this situation?'
'What would your friend say to you in this situation?'
'What would you say to your friend if they were in your situation?'

Using Scales

Scales are an excellent tool for assisting the coachee to create strategies and decide their next steps (Greene and Grant 2003). Scales can be used in a variety of situations:

- To highlight and measure progress.
- To illustrate to the coachee how much they have achieved, when they are experiencing a setback.
- To understand how the coachee feels in relation to other situations.

The easiest scale to use is a scale of 1 to 10, 1 being low and 10 being high. You could say, 'on a scale of 1 to 10, 1 being low and 10 being high, how assertive are you at work?' They might say a 4. You could then ask 'What would a 6 look like? What would people notice about you if you were at a 6? How would you be behaving?'

If discussing a negative situation you could say, 'on a scale of one to ten, how well did you cope? They might well say zero. Then you might say, 'how come you were not minus 1? They may well reply with 'I was minus 1'. You can reply with 'Okay so you say you were minus 1. How come you were not minus 2? How did you cope? What did you do that prevented the situation from escalating?'

Consider some situations where you might use scales within your coaching sessions.

Maintaining A Positive Focus

Coaching benefits from using positive psychology and maintaining a positive focus. The coach can investigate with the coachee what is going well, what is working well and what is improving. The coach can re-frame situations positively, which will help to reduce the coachee's negative emotions (Kraft et al 1985). Positive emotions can be a great catalyst to change (Fitzpatrick 2008).

Using this positive psychological approach has also been shown to reduce stress levels, generate greater self-esteem and improve well-being (Wood et al 2011).

Using a positive approach will naturally motivate the individual. It will also help to increase their confidence, making them more likely to attempt their action plan. It reinforces what the coachee did well. Discussing situations where the client has enjoyed success helps them to identify which thought patterns and behaviours were helpful. With this clear focus the coachee can integrate more of the successful behaviours and reduce the less successful behaviours. This will ultimately lead to greater levels of success.

The positive approach focuses on what the coachee is doing right, which makes for a positive coaching session. As the coaching sessions are a positive experience, it is likely the coachee will wish to partake in further sessions.

If the coachee has experienced a failure of some kind, you need to remove the failure aspects. When people feel they have failed in the past, it can make them fearful of trying a similar task in the future. The individual might recall the failure as psychologically upsetting and fear experiencing similar emotions once again. Their negative thought-patterns can cause low levels of confidence, low levels of self-esteem and an unwillingness to try anything new. This can prevent them from achieving their full potential. These negative thought patterns can be difficult for the individual to change. The role of the coach is to try to change their perspective on the failure.

A football team has lost three consecutive matches……

The team are focusing on the negative elements of the match and analysing what went wrong. As a result of this approach certain individuals are being blamed for the loss. What do you think would be mindset regarding the next game?

Whilst a few individuals might use the lack of success as a motivator and remain determined to win this match, many of the players will feel deflated. They will likely believe there is a strong chance they are going to lose.

Now consider, they review each match and discuss what went wrong but also what they could do better in the future. What do you think their mindset would be before the next game?

The majority would likely feel both positive and negative emotions about the match. They might still be thinking about their previous mistakes which could impact their performance.

Now consider they looked at what went wrong, what they could do better, but they also now look at what did work and what was right? How do you think they would feel before the next game? What would their mindset be? Compare this to how they would feel if they only considered what went wrong.

The focus on the positives of the game would likely result in more positive attitudes compared to when they were focusing on the negative aspects of the game. Positive attitudes make success more likely.

Whilst this example relates to sporting psychology it is exactly the same in an organisational setting. Looking at what the individual is doing right can lead to a positive attitude, making success more likely.

When a coachee is talking about an event they consider to be a failure, you aim is to help them identify the positive aspects.

You might ask:
What did work?

What did you do right?

What did you do that prevented events from escalating further?

Activity

Think of a situation where you consider yourself to have failed, or to not have been as successful as you hoped. Note down how you feel about the situation in as many words as you feel appropriate.

Still thinking about the same situation note down: What did you do well? What did work? What aspects were you pleased with? What did you do that prevented the situation from being worse?

Repeat the process two more times with different personal examples. This will help you to pull the positive elements out of considered failures. You can then use this skill to help your coachees.

Now consider how you originally felt about the failures. Have your feelings changed, even if only slightly?

Summarising and Providing Feedback

Sometimes it can be useful to summarise back to the coachee what you have just heard. This has two benefits. Firstly, it shows that you are listening. Secondly, when a coachee hears their own thoughts presented back to them, it can make them change their perspective. It can provide them with clarity. You might start the summary with 'Okay, so you feel that…….' or 'In your experience you have found that...' . People can have blind-spots where they are not aware of their own behaviour. When receiving a summary of what they have just said, these blind-spots can suddenly be seen. These can then be explored further by the coach's questioning.

Another important aspect of the coaching situation is providing feedback. There are a few rules that are helpful to adhere to. Feedback should be honest and straight forward. It is important that it focuses on behaviour and not personality traits. When providing feedback ensure that you use specific examples of behaviour to make your point, as opposed to generalisations. By providing specific examples the coachee is more likely to accept your feedback and be able to use it to change their future behaviour.

Activity

Think of a person within your team. Consider what feedback you could give them. Using the key points discussed, write a short transcript of how you would phrase the feedback. This will help the techniques to become more natural.

Looking for Patterns

People are often unaware of their habitual thinking patterns and behaviours. These patterns can result in either positive or negative outcomes for the individual.

In order to assist the coachee with identifying patterns in their thoughts or behaviours, the coach can ask them if they have experienced a similar situation in the past. The coachee can then discuss this situation in as little, or as much, depth as they like. Once the coachee has finished speaking the coach can summarise the situation back to the coachee. The coachee may well find that hearing their story reflected back to them highlights their habitual responses.

As an example, you could ask 'Have there been occasions in the past when you were assertive?' or 'Has there been a situation in the past when you have had to manage change?'

In your role as coach, you need to ask the coachee about their thoughts and behaviours however it is not necessary to know the fine details of a situation.

You can ask them various questions to help them learn from the past, such as asking what worked and what didn't. Exploring similar events in the coachee's past can help to identify what works for them and what hinders their progress.

Imagine you are the coach and the coachee you are working with has been trying to improve their assertiveness skills. In this coaching session they tell you that during a recent meeting they remained silent, even though they strongly disagreed with the plan the group was creating.

The coachee is feeling they have failed. The questions you could ask are: 'Did you speak at the meeting? What did you say?' You would try to find examples of when they did put forward their ideas. You could then ask 'What made you feel confident enough to speak at that moment? 'What helped?' 'Has there been a meeting in the past where you did speak about your views?' 'What helped you to speak your views? 'How can you use this knowledge to help you voice your thoughts in the future? Asking these questions will help the coachee identify the thoughts they have when they are feeling confident and able to be assertive.

Hopefully the coachee will be able to notice the patterns in their thoughts themselves. However, sometimes further questioning is required. If you have been working with a coachee for a period of time, you might be able to highlight a previous example they have given you in order to help them identify the pattern.

Activity
Consider either a skill area you would like to develop or a certain type of situation you would like to manage better. Consider your past behaviour and see if you can identify any patterns in your thoughts or behaviours. Note any questions that you ask yourself in order to help identify the patterns. You can use these questions to assist your coachees in identifying their habitual thought patterns and behaviours.

Transferring what is working elsewhere.

Another technique is to ask what is working elsewhere and to see if these techniques can be applied to the current situation. This is particularly useful when investigating possible solutions to problems or challenges that the coachee is facing. Highlighting success in other areas of the client's life can also increase the coachee's confidence levels when they are thinking about attempting their next steps.

People often find themselves with a recurring problem. In many cases this is due to the fact that they keep using the same or similar solutions. Usually this is because they are uncertain as to what else they can try. However, as the famous saying goes 'If you always do what you have always done, you will always get, what you have always got'.

A solution-focused, positive approach that builds on the coachee's strengths can assist in breaking habitual thought patterns and behaviours (Palmer and Whybrow 2007).

As an example, let's consider a coachee who wants to improve their presentation skills. They have completed a training course, yet still lack the confidence to deliver a presentation. As a coach you could ask them 'Are there other areas in your working life where you have to verbally present information to others?' 'Are there any other areas in your working life where you have to teach others how to complete a certain task?' 'Do you ever have to try to change people's viewpoints in your working life?' 'What techniques do you use on these occasions?' 'What works well?' 'Could you transfer the skills you already have into the new presentations?'

Reading the Coachee

It is vital that you monitor the coachee's behaviour as it can help you identify when your questions are making the coachee uncomfortable. The key is to look for **changes** in their behaviour. Reading body language and eye contact can be misleading. It is the changes that are the most important. For example, the coachee might have been sitting still for most of the session and then starts to appear uncomfortable and restless. Perhaps they were giving you eye contact and then they start to suddenly avoid your eye. These changes could indicate there might be a problem. Alternatively, they might suddenly try to change the subject.

If they appear to be feeling uncomfortable, ease off the subject and take it back to the previous level.

Activity
Think of three people you consider to be good listeners. Do not move on until you have three definite people in mind.

Different Levels of Listening

When we do this exercise in our public training courses it can take some delegates up to 5 minutes to think of three people. Our delegates are often surprised at how difficult they found it to think of three good listeners. This is particularly interesting as most people consider themselves to be a good listener.

Look back at your list of three people. Are any of them disliked by you? Are they loved by you? Are they respected by you? People who are good listeners are usually liked or loved by others. If they are not liked or loved, they at least have other people's respect. This shows how important listening is.

There are different levels of listening.

Cosmetic Listening – Appears to be listening yet is actually just remaining silent and waiting for their turn to speak.

Conversational Listening – Engaging in the conversation, listening, talking and thinking the subject through.

Active Listening – Giving full attention to the conversation and trying to fully comprehend the content. Developing suitable questions to ask to further their understanding.

Deep Listening – Focusing more on the other person than themselves and trying to understand the other person's perspective, values, beliefs, habitual thinking patterns and behaviours. Deep listening is particularly effective in the coaching situation.

Consider which of the following you tend to do while listening:
Do you pretend to listen, whilst thinking about other things?
Do you finish the other person sentences?
Do you avoid listening to stories that are long and difficult to follow?
Do you judge the words that people choose?
Do you predict what the other person will say?
Do you suddenly realise mid-conversation that you have switched off and not been listening?
Do you interrupt the speaker to clarify the situation?
Do you reply with your own story before fully investigating what the other person has to say?

All of the actions above are examples of ineffective listening.

Ethical Issues in Coaching

There are various ethical issues to consider when coaching:

Confidentiality must be upheld.

Sometimes during a coaching session, you might discover that the coachee is showing warning signs of a more serious problem. If this is the case, you need to signpost them to relevant support services that are trained to manage the situation.

Ensure the goals they set are realistic. If they try and fail, they may experience lower self-esteem and lower levels of confidence. This could have long lasting effects and impact considerably on their future.

Know when to stop or change direction of the coaching session. If you notice a change in the coachee and suspect they are feeling uncomfortable with your questioning, take a break or move on to discuss a different aspect.

Sometimes it can be inappropriate to use coaching or coaching questions. If somebody is experiencing a change of some kind, it is important they naturally grieve for the losses. Pushing coaching and a positive attitude too soon would not be appropriate in this situation. They need time to adjust and accept the situation first.

Ensure that you are not trying to provide counselling to the individual. You do not need to know WHY.

In Summary

Coaching aims to give the coachee time to think and solve their own problems. Your role is to ask questions which will challenge their thoughts and assist them to develop strategies.

At the start of the session identify the goal. This might be an overall goal or a smaller goal for the session.

Use 'What questioning' to identify and explore the problem, aid implementation, help them make decisions, check if there are any influences, create motivation and encourage action.

Use the technique of 'what else' and 'what difference would that make' to help the coachee develop further options and understand their motivation. Use constructive feedback and summarise back to them what you have heard. Try to help them identify patterns. Always maintain a positive focus.

Wrap up the session, using a summary of what has been discussed. Usually during a coaching session, you will have discussed what the coachee's next steps might be. Remind them of these. Agree on what they might work on between now and the next session. Ensure their goals are SMART – specific, measurable, achievable, realistic and timed.

Sometimes it can be quite daunting to start coaching individuals or your team. Common fears include feeling unsure of which questions to ask and when. However, once you start you will find the questions will naturally flow. To practise you can start asking the odd coaching question to your employees. Try to follow up their answer with another coaching question.

Understanding Stress

If someone asked you 'What is Stress?', how would you explain it? Take a few minutes to consider your thoughts before reading on.

What is Stress?

The word 'Stress' originates from the Latin word 'stringere' which means 'to be drawn tight'. Stress was first recognised as having a long-term affect on health in 1929 by Walter B. Cannon.

When confronted with extreme danger people choose whether to stay and 'fight', or run away which is termed 'flight'. A researcher called Cannon was one of the first researchers to discover that in these situations people experience physiological changes such as emergency adrenalin secretions. Cannon considered these individuals to be 'under stress'.

Stress often occurs when an individual does not have the resources to deal with the particular situation or environment they find themselves in. Cummings and Cooper (1979) suggest that individuals try to keep their thoughts, emotions and relationships with others in a 'steady state'.

Individuals have a range of stability where they feel comfortable. They can cope with changes to a certain degree. If a change occurs which forces them beyond their comfort zone, they will feel distressed. The individual has to work to restore a feeling of calm either through taking action or employing a coping strategy.

Let's imagine an individual experiences a threat and subsequently feels stress. If they are able to manage this threat by taking action or adopting certain copy strategies, they will return to a steady state and no longer feel stress. Whereas, if they do NOT have adequate processes or coping strategies they basically 'fail to cope'. They will experience continued stress (Cooper 1996).

If it is perceived that an event is likely to occur that will cause stress, a threat exists. A threat alone can cause stress.

Stress can cause various symptoms in the body and mind. The medical profession have identified various physical and behavioural symptoms of stress. These symptoms can lead to further health implications or aggravate other ailments.

Physical Symptoms of Stress

Various studies have concluded the following physical symptoms:

Nausea
Indigestion/Heartburn
Bowel problems
Fatigue
Headaches
Dizziness
Reduced appetite and subsequent weight loss
Weight gain from comfort eating
Disturbed sleep patterns
Shaking
Nervous twitches
Sweating
High blood pressure

Ailments Aggravated Or Brought On By Stress

Many ailments are aggravated by stress. It might be that a physical problem (non-stress related) is made worse by stress. For example, food intolerance, if left untreated, may cause the individual to experience frequent or even constant indigestion. If the individual concerned feels a certain level of stress, the stress aggravates the indigestion and results in a worsening of the original symptoms.

The Word 'Stress'

The effect of saying the words 'I am stressed' can actually make a person feel more stressed. The word stress is used very broadly. It covers anything unpleasant that happens (Arnold 2005). People use the word 'stress' for example, to describe how they are feeling regarding a colleague's behaviour. They then use the same word 'stress' to describe how they are feeling about their divorce.

Sometimes it is not useful to use the word as it can hide the real problem. Many counsellors ban the word stress as it is too generic and not a useful word when trying to identify the causes of distress.

Most people associate negative connotations with the word 'stress'. However, low levels of stress can actually be a positive experience, creating challenge and subsequent satisfaction. We can experience stress and positive emotions at the same time for example, when we work on our personal development. Whilst this is a positive event, it can make us feel stressed as it also a challenge. Certain job roles can be stressful, yet also satisfying and rewarding. Positive stress is sometimes referred to as 'Eustress' (Seyle 1975).

Perceptions of Stress

People perceive stress differently. One person might describe themselves as 'stressed' whereas another person, with exactly the same feelings, would not consider themselves to be stressed. In addition, the way people perceive situations affects the amount of 'stress' they experience.

Different events cause different levels of stress in people. One person may feel stressed if they are queuing in a shop whereas another person may feel calm. Individuals may find a situation causes them stress one day, yet another day it does not.

Behavioural Habits

Some individuals appear to experience constant stress in their lives. They regularly complain to others how stressful their lives are. For some people it becomes part of their identity.

Stress Culture

In some teams or organisations, the employees regularly complain about their stress levels. These conversations allow the employees to vent their feelings however, unfortunately the conversations do not lead to constructive plans to address the stresses. People are 'stressed' and it becomes almost a competitive situation of who is the most stressed. Stress is accepted as normal and a person who is not experiencing or showing stress seems the odd one out. It might even be perceived that because they do not appear stressed, they do not have enough work on or they do not care enough.

This can be very detrimental to an organisation's atmosphere as emotions are contagious. Stress is infectious, as is calmness.

Activity
Consider situations in the past where others around you have displayed positive and negative emotions. Consider the impact this had on the rest of the group. Which emotions do you think are transferred with more ease and speed, positive or negative?

Comment
Research has shown that negative emotions are transferred with more ease and speed.

Activity
Think about situations in the past where there was a negative or positive working environment. Who was the person with the most power? Did the negative or positive working environment reflect their general mood or persona? Do you think the person with the most power affects the atmosphere more than the other team members?

Comment

People who are in power are more 'infectious', in that their emotions pass quicker to others. When we talk about power we are not always talking about the person who has the most senior position. A person in a lower position can hold more power. If the manager lacks confidence and fails to control situations, it often results in another team member taking control and therefore having more power than the manager.

The Costs of Organisational Stress

Latest estimates from the Labour Force Survey (LFS), quoted by Health Safety Executive (HSE) 2013:

40% of all work-related illnesses in 2011/2012 were due to stress. 428 000 cases out of 1 073 000 were stress related. This resulted in 10.4 million working days lost, based on LFS data. Larger organisations tended to see more working days lost due to this condition, rather than small to medium sized business.

Stress leads to high absenteeism, high labour turnover, more accidents, more mistakes and creativity/productivity can be threatened.

Causes of Stress at Work

Most job roles have elements which can cause the employee to experience stress. Employees can experience stress regardless of the seniority of their job role.

An entry level role has stressors and whilst they are perhaps different stressors to a more senior role, the stressors will impact on mental well-being and subsequently on physical health.

Researchers have identified seven major sources of work stress (Cooper et al 1988, Sutherland and Cooper 2000):

1. Factors intrinsic to the job.

2. Role in the organisation.

3. Personality and coping strategy.

4. Relationships at work.

5. Career development.

6. Organisational culture and climate.

7. Home and work conflict.

Activity
Write a list of situations which have caused you to feel stressed at work. Next, categorise your list using the seven sources of work stress as suggested by Cooper et al (1988), and Sutherland and Cooper (2000). Note if there is a particular category that has caused you stress more often than the others. Next note the severity of stress that you experienced for each category.

Comment
Although the stressors can be neatly put into seven categories, the categories are very broad. People may find certain categories of stressor

more distressing than others. People differ in what they find most distressing. This activity helps to highlight the large scope of stress at work and its many various sources.

Sources of workplace stress vary in the extent that they trigger a stress response. The LFS survey investigated the causes of stress using a self-report measure. They discovered that the top three main work activities which caused work related stress (averaged over 2009/10-2011/12) were:

1. Workload. This included too much work, pressure, responsibility or tight deadlines.

2. Lack of managerial support.

3. Violence, threats and bullying.

The GP reporting network (THOR) collates information from GPs across Great Britain regarding work related diseases. The patients suffering with work-related stress identified the following factors as the cause of their stress (Source: HSE website, 2013):

1. Fundamental elements of the role including the pressure of the job and inadequate support from managers.

2. Changes at work, which included other staff leaving the company and subsequent changes in their roles.

3. Interpersonal relationships at work such as bullying and relationships with managers.

The current economic climate has put additional stress on workers. These include:

- Threat of redundancy
- Staff shortages
- Increased workload and tighter deadlines. This can reduce quality of work, reduce time for breaks, affect concentration and increase working hours.

- Lack of training for the changes that occur to their roles (often as a result of other employees being made redundant).
- Pay freezes, reduction in bonuses and lack of career progression opportunities.
- Poor working environments. As money is tight some organisations don't have the funds to spend on the working environment, resulting in poor repair.
- Home life and the financial pressures impacting on the stress a person feels at work.

Activity

Take some time to have a think about the stressors people may be experiencing in your organisation

- as a whole organisation
- in your team
- as individuals

Note that a stressor for a particular individual may not be a stressor for the whole team.

We are now going to look at the major work stressors in turn. Firstly we are going to consider the stressor of 'Factors Intrinsic to the Job'.

Factors Intrinsic To The Job

Poor Working Environment – The physical working environment can impact on how we feel. This can include noise levels, smells, lighting and aesthetic appeal. This can occur even if we do not find them consciously unsettling.

Shift Work - Shift work can have an impact on sleep patterns, appetite and body temperature particularly if working nights (Tucker and Knowles 2008).

Long Hours and Work Overload - Long hours and work overload are a major source of health problems. The impact can be moderated if the individual has a choice regarding the working of such hours (Tucker and Rutherford 2005).

Work Under-load - Work under-load is often not considered when we initially think about what might be causing people stress. Work tasks may be repetitive and unchallenging. Work under-load is also linked to ill health (Cox 1980, Sutherland and Cooper 2000).

Emails, Technology and 24/7 Contact - When working on a task, individuals may feel the need to constantly check and read emails. This can result in tasks taking far longer than they would normally. The constant interruptions result in the individual spending additional time re-focusing their attention on the task. As work tasks take longer, it can increase pressure particularly if the current or subsequent work tasks have associated deadlines.

With the invention of technology people can access work 24/7. Many employees check work emails in the evening and as a result are often unable to relax. If, for example, a person reads a distressing email in the evening at home, they will worry about it until work the next day. With emails being quick and easy to send, many employees find they receive many that are not relevant to them.

Travel - Travel is often overlooked when looking at causes of workplace stress. Commuting can be a stressful event and this can seep into the work day. Long periods away from home can also have a substantial impact.

How to reduce stress caused by Factors Intrinsic To The Job:

Many of the intrinsic factors of the role cannot be changed. However a few aspects that can be altered are:

Encourage employees to focus solely on a work task for one to two hours. During this time encourage them not to check phones or emails. Ideally, they would also not be disturbed by colleagues. Organisations that allow for this quiet time often see increases in productivity.

Regularly assess whether your employees are at risk of work under-load or over-load. Job rotation can be considered for boring repetitive jobs. It is advisable to talk to employees regarding how they feel about job rotation before enforcing it. Some employees may be against the idea and this in itself could raise stress levels.

Role In The Organisation

Employees whose roles are ambiguous or conflicting can experience lower job satisfaction, increased anxiety and increased stress levels. It can lead to cardiovascular ill health risks, such as elevated blood pressure and abnormal blood chemistry (Ivancevich and Matteson 1980). Workers are often heard saying, 'I'm not doing that, it's not my job. It's not in my job description!' Workers can often feel torn between two different groups of people who are demanding different tasks from them.

A wide range of events can cause role ambiguity. These include changes in staffing. If an employee leaves and their post is not immediately taken over by a new employee, work tasks are often shared out amongst other team members. Ambiguity also arises in organisational restructuring, new management, organisational growth and non-specific job descriptions. Individuals are unsure of their responsibilities or the expectations of their role by others.

How to reduce stress caused by Role:

Roles need to be clearly defined. Employees can feel frustrated when they are allocated tasks that they believe are not in their job description. Encouraging flexibility from the outset allows for unforeseen roles that may be required of them in the future.

As organisation changes occur ensure employees are aware of any new 'expectations'.

Ensure new work tasks are explained in detail.

Ensure new responsibilities do not create complications with current work tasks.

Make sure individuals understand their role and responsibilities.

Encourage employees to raise concerns about new responsibilities.

Personality and Coping

The level of stress a person experiences is moderated by their personality style and coping strategies (Connor-Smith & Flachsbart 2007). For example, individuals who accept change easily are more likely to respond to stressors such as new role responsibilities with less tension than somebody who is change resistant.

An employee who was naturally extraverted would enjoy a social working environment. If the same person was to carry out a role that was socially isolating, they may begin to experience some degree of stress.

Another factor is the '**locus of control**'. This relates to how much a person believes they have control over their own life. Someone who believes they have large amounts of control may suffer less stress as they naturally take action on the stressor. This is fine unless there really is nothing they can do about their situation. They might then find this lack of control particularly stressful.

In addition there are Type A and Type B personalities. Type A personalities are more prone to stress (Rosenman et al 1964). Here is a list of type A behaviours, (type B would be the opposite):

Doesn't like to be late

Finishes other peoples sentences for them

Always trying to do things as quickly as possible

Impatient

Multitasks

While doing one thing, their mind is thinking about other tasks that need to be completed

Speaks quickly

Desires recognition and praise for achievements

Always wants to achieve more

Pushes others to achieve more

Highly ambitious

Tends to hide feelings from others

Has few hobbies that are outside of work or the home

People may display some Type A traits and some Type B traits, however most will tend towards either a Type A or a Type B.

How to reduce stress caused by Personality and Coping Abilities:

Relieve anxieties through clear communication.

Regularly provide information regarding any upcoming changes. Reiterate changes. Telling employees once is rarely enough. To avoid being repetitive you can provide the information in different formats e.g. newsletters, meetings, notice boards etc. Providing clear information regularly can dispel anxiety provoking rumours. Inform employees of estimated timescales.

Ask if employees feel able to roll out the changes required. If they are not comfortable with any of the changes or feel unable to carry out their new responsibilities, provide them with additional support. This could include formal training, mentoring or coaching.

Relationships At Work

Relationships with Managers. If an employee does not have a positive working relationship with their manager, it can cause them to feel stressed. Poor relationships exhibit a low level of trust and low supportiveness. Managers can cause their team members to feel stressed as a result of numerous different actions. These include lack of active listening, lack of support, micro-managing, aggressive leadership style, threatening comments or not leading by example. Some managers, for example, might be strict on lateness, yet arrive late themselves without explanation.

An inspirational leadership style can reduce the stress felt by individuals (Sosik and Godshalk 2000). This 'inspirational leadership' consists of meeting the individual's needs, assisting their development, being a strong role model and portraying a clear vision of the future for the employee.

Relationships with team members. It might be that as a manager you find the relationship with a team member causes you stress. Alternatively an individual within your team may experience stress supervising others.

Relationships with Colleagues. Relationship stress can also exist between team members. Stress can occur as a result of different personality types, work load, task responsibility, rewards and promotions.

Relationships at work can either be a source of distress or act as a buffer for stress. Positive relationships can greatly reduce perceived stress levels (Lazurus 1966).

1 in 4 people consider themselves bullied in the workplace (Samaritans 2008). Bullying can take many forms in the workplace. An employee may be obviously aggressive to another employee. Alternatively, they may be more subtle and act passive aggressively towards them. Either way, the continual friction can create a mounting level of stress. One thing to bear in mind is that bullying can be unintentional.

In a large scale study of union members in the UK (UNISON 1997) 9 out of 10 people agreed with the statements that bullying exists in the workplace because 'the bully can get away with it' and the targets are 'too afraid to report it'.

Workplace bullying can consist of the following behaviours:

- Spreading rumours
- Talking negatively about an individual not present
- Isolating an individual
- Making comments about the state of individual's mental health
- Giving an individual the simple, routine tasks
- Criticising an individual
- Failure to provide recognition for achievements
- Removing responsibility with no valid reasoning
- Ignoring an individual
- Disregarding an individual's suggestions or viewpoints

If the above behaviours occur regularly, the targeted individual may feel they are being bullied.

How to reduce stress caused by Relationships at Work:

If you know relationships are strained, do not ignore them. Discuss the situation with both parties. It might become apparent that the conflict is arising from something simple such as work task allocation or responsibilities. These can be fairly easily solved through clearly specifying individual responsibilities.

Encourage positive interactions. Act as a positive role model.

Encourage all employees to share information relevant to the work. Create systems if necessary.

Encourage employees to inform you of any workplace bullying and take steps to manage the situation. Put preventative measures in place if necessary.

Career Development

Career Development is another stressor.

Career Progression - People generally enjoy developing their professional abilities and striving for the next level. An employee may experience stress if they feel they are unable to progress any further in their career (Ivancevich and Matteson 1980).

Retirement - Some people find the prospect of retiring stressful.

Job Performance –Many workplaces monitor and assess employees' performance which can increase stress levels. However, so can not being appraised.

How to reduce stress caused by Career Development factors:

Ensure people are regularly appraised. Ensure both positive and constructive feedback is provided. People can only take in a few pieces of negative feedback at a time. Anymore than this and they can start to feel deflated, de-motivated and may experience lower self-esteem.

Individuals who have reached their career ceiling or are due to retire, may enjoy coaching and mentoring others in the workplace. It can provide them with a renewed motivation as they focus on sharing their knowledge with others.

Organisational Culture and Climate

Another one of the seven factors that causes stress at work is the organisational culture and climate. Organisational culture and climate can either cause stress or it can act as a buffer to it.

Organisational culture and climate refers to the way of life of the organisation. It refers to the collective values, beliefs and behaviours of the employees.

Activity
Are there any aspects of your organisation's culture and climate that may cause stress levels to rise in some people? Can these be changed in any way?

Are there any aspects of it which act as a buffer to the stresses of working life? How can you ensure these buffers are maintained?

Home and Work Conflicts

The final stressor is home and work conflict. The time pressures between the two can cause high stress levels. This can be further exacerbated in tough economic times. Organisations when short staffed often require the remaining staff to take on extra work. This often results in longer hours for no more reward. People who fear losing their jobs may work longer hours to try to secure them. This puts further pressure on their home life. In addition home life can be fraught with financial concerns and this stress seeps into their working life often impacting their performance.

Activity
Look back at the suggestions for reducing stress from the different

stressors. Using this as a guide, consider what you are already doing that helps to create a positive work environment.

Develop an action plan as to how you could further improve your work environment. When developing your plan, take into consideration your role and be realistic regarding the changes you are able to make.

Managing Stress

Problem Solving Framework

We are going to look at the Problem Solving Framework as a way of managing workplace stress. When an individual is stressed, they are more likely to experience 'tunnel vision'. Problem solving techniques help the individual or group create a variety of possible solutions. It increases the likelihood of a successful outcome (D'Zurilla and Goldfried 1971).

Problem solving techniques help to refocus the attention away from problems and into considered action plans (Jia-ShengHeh 1999).Having a planned solution, whether it is changing the stressor or learning to cope with it, reduces stress levels. Problem solving helps to improve mental and physical health (Malouff et al 2007).

The Problem Solving Framework (Cartwright and Cooper 1997) can be used as an action plan for managing stress in the workplace:

1. Be aware that a problem exists.

2. Try to clarify the problem or discover the underlying stressor.

3. Aim to find a solution which solves the problem or changes the stressor.

4. If the problem/stressor cannot be changed, then develop coping strategies.

5. Monitor and evaluate progress.

We are going to look at each of these steps in turn.

1. Be Aware That a Problem Exists

Recognising and accepting that a problem exists is the obvious first step towards finding a solution. At times it can feel easier to ignore situations that feel uncomfortable.

General organisational/team stress can be monitored in a variety of behavioural indices: employee turnover, number of missed workdays due to sickness, number of accidents, insurance claims, employee satisfaction surveys and relations generally.

There are also various indicators that indicate an individual might be suffering with stress. What indicators are there? What do you currently look for?

The more indicators an individual displays, the higher the risk of elevated stress levels. However, it is the changes in people's behaviours that are the most important indicator. If the individual concerned is always sensitive, it does not mean they are stressed. However, if they suddenly start appearing more sensitive, it could be an indicator of increased stress levels.

Performance Indicators:

Lower performance levels

Difficulty making decisions

Poor concentration

Forgetfulness

Reduced commitment

Increased number of mistakes

Working longer hours

Not taking permitted annual leave or toil

Negative Behavioural Indicators:

Increased tearfulness

Appears more sensitive

Irritable

Sudden changes in mood

Less patient

Easily frustrated

Prone to over-reactions

Sulking

Disengagement Indicators:

Poor timekeeping compared to normal

Increased number of sick days or using up annual leave early

Lack of interest

Lack of motivation

Not socialising with other colleagues

Negative Interpersonal Indicators:

Talking negatively about other colleagues

Being quick to judge and criticise others

Increased level of aggression towards others

Increased irritability

Conflicts with colleagues

Behavioural Change Indicators:

Eating more or less

Increased negative thoughts, perspectives or behaviours

Increased intake of alcohol

Reduced levels of personal hygiene

Increased risk taking behaviours

Increased activity with the apparent inability to relax

Physical Indicators:

Nervousness

Overheating and excessive sweating

Regular stomach problems

Regular bowel problems

Regular headaches

Dizziness

Fatigue and exhaustion

2. Try to clarify the problem or discover the underlying stressor

The next step is to try to identify and isolate the stressor or stressors. It may be that you can identify what you think the possible stressors might be from the Causes of Workplace Stress section of this book. Alternatively you might be unaware of the cause. Ideally, you would discuss the causes of stress with the employee.

If you have noticed an employee appears to be stressed and they have not raised any concerns with you, you need to speak with them. This is a delicate situation and could exacerbate the problem.

Activity

Imagine one of your employees appears to be struggling at work. There have been a few occasions recently where they have appeared tearful as a result of conversations with both you and other colleagues.

This is unlike them. They seem distant and agitated. They have stopped socialising with other colleagues and appear to be eating far less than usual. They appear tired and drawn. This has been getting steadily worse over the past month and you think they **might** be suffering with stress. Consider how you would manage this situation.

Would you approach them?

How would you approach them?

What are the risks?

The next section will look at the best way to approach the situation. Consider which of these elements you had thought of and what else you could add to your answer.

Once you have identified some unusual or worrying aspect of behaviour, it is important to find out more information. You need to try and discover what is causing the problem and consider what changes, if any, can be implemented to resolve the issue. Ensure you use a matter of fact, straight forward approach. Be careful not to over exaggerate the situation.

Ensure the employee remains in control of the conversation. It is up to the employee how much they wish to tell you, if anything at all. After the employee has finished their sentence, you can use silence of up to 5 seconds to allow the employee to share more with you if they wish to. Be careful not to cut off the conversation by interrupting them or providing advice. This is the time to solely listen.

Ask questions which allow for the individual to say as much or as little as they like. For example:

I've noticed that you are working longer hours than normal, is your workload okay?

I've noticed that you haven't been coming out to the team lunches recently, is everything okay?

Is there anything that is concerning you at work at the moment?

You might get a one word answer. If that's the case, you could try remaining silent for a few moments. This allows the person to provide more information, should they wish to. If they do not elaborate on their answer, the person is clearly not ready to discuss the issue with you.

Never push for an answer as this may cause the individual to close down further. Show patience. If they do decide to share their thoughts with you, you do not need to ask further questions in order to discover the finer details. You only require enough information in order to be able to offer assistance.

Avoid phrases that diagnose the person for example 'I think you are suffering with work-related stress' or 'I think you might be suffering with depression'. Instead say, 'You seem a little less enthusiastic about the job lately'.

Acknowledge the mood or behaviour rather than diagnosing.

Activity
Consider occasions when you have used the word 'stressed'. If the word 'stressed' did not exist what would you had said instead? Think of friends or family who have uttered the phrase 'I am stressed'. What would they have said instead if the word did not exist?

The word 'stress' risks hiding important differences between different types of negative events and emotions.

Two different people may say 'I am stressed at work'. If they had to replace the word stress, one might say 'I am worried because I have too much work to do'. The other person might say 'I am unhappy at work because I am not getting along with my colleagues.' Removing the word stress can help to identify the cause of workplace stress. This is sometimes used as a counselling technique. The person being counselled is asked to tell the counsellor what the problem is but to avoid using the word stress. This helps the person to gain clarity over the situation and solutions are easier to discover. You may decide to use this technique if it seems appropriate during initial or subsequent discussions.

Another way to uncover the cause of the stressor is a technique called the 'Five Why's.' This technique helps to discover what is causing the stress and can even highlight a potential solution. The Five Why's can appear a little odd to an employee who is not expecting it. You can mention to the employee that you will be using a technique called the 'Five Why's' to discover what the problem is and to possibly identify a solution. Look at the example below.

Employee: I feel stressed.

Manager: Why?

Employee: Because I'm arguing with my colleagues.

Manager: Why?

Employee: Because we are struggling to figure out who is responsible for the different aspects of the client's project.

Manager: Why do you think this is happening?

Employee: I don't know. I suppose we haven't sat down and allocated the tasks out.

Manager: Why?

Employee: Because it all feels a bit awkward, I guess.

Manager: Why?

Employee: Because there is no obvious person to lead the meeting. Maybe it needs to be led by the manager?

The manager in this example can then hold a meeting to allocate the different work tasks.

3. Attempt to change the stressor

4. If the problem/stressor cannot be changed, then develop coping strategies

Once the stressor is identified you need to work with the employee to change or manage the problem. Active steps should be taken that are known to reduce the problem (from the Causes of Workplace Stress section). Some things cannot be changed and therefore have to be coped with. Some organisations have counselling or coaching schemes which can help employees to manage problems or stressors that cannot be changed. Regular discussions with the employee can help if time permits.

Activity
If a stressor cannot be changed, what can a manager do to assist the employee to cope?

Comment
As a manager you can encourage strong social networks as these help to reduce stress. Ensure relationships are happy in the office. A positive working environment can act as a buffer to stress. Be aware that emotions are contagious and acting as a positive role model can increase positivity in the workplace. Demonstrating how you successfully manage stresses in the workplace can assist your team members with their own stress management techniques. Ensure they feel free to talk to you.

5. Monitor and evaluate progress

The final stage is to monitor and review the outcome. On an organisation/group level you could monitor employee turnover, number of missed workdays due to sickness, number of accidents, insurance claims, employee satisfaction surveys and relations generally.

On an individual level, monitor the situation regularly. Take the time to ask if the situation remains the same or is improving. This reminds the employee that you are concerned for their wellbeing. Even if the stressor has been resolved, checking that it is still okay can make a big difference. This can keep communications open and therefore problems can be resolved quickly before they escalate.

Activity
Reflect on a past experience when you felt that somebody within your team was suffering from stress. Using the ideas in this book:

What stress indicators did the individual display?

Plan how you would have approached the individual. What would you have said?

What techniques would you have used to identify the stressor?

What plans would you subsequently have made to either change the stressor or help the person manage the stressor?

How would you have reviewed or monitored the outcome?

This activity will help you to review the whole process.

Change Management

Types of Change

There are two different types of change, planned and emergent. In the 1940's Kurt Lewin developed the notion of planned change. He suggested that change is deliberately planned and subsequently embarked upon in organisations (Marrow 1977). They can move from one stable state to another in a pre-planned manner.

Emergent change does not see change as a planned event, instead it views change as a continuous process. This a more realistic view of how many workplaces experience change in today's climate. If you can encourage your employees to view change as the norm, they will be far more receptive to changes you introduce in the workplace.

Five Laws of Organisation Development

There are five laws of organisation development in relation to workplace change or transition:

1. An individual may cope well with the changes initially but this could change at any moment. At the beginning of the change programme, the individual might have appeared to be coping well with the changes, however, as time progresses the continued uncertainty is straining their personal resources.

2. Successful outcomes will no doubt encourage challenge. Success leads to change. Change can be challenging whether it is considered positive or negative. The organisation might not have the resources to manage the changes. This is often seen when a company undergoes rapid growth.

3. The underlying factors that resulted in its success may now be causing its demise. Organisations often outgrow their current processes forcing changes to occur.

4. Usually troubled times = developmental change. When an organisation is experiencing troubled times, it is usually because there is a need for change in order to adapt to the new situation. Alternatively, a change process might already be taking place.

5. Not recognising or engaging with the need for change. Organisations need to future proof their product or services. Not moving with the times can leave the competition with a clear advantage.

Transition Management Process – Involving the Employees

It is important that organisations ensure people are involved in the transition management process as it helps to support the new beginning by:

1. Ensuring the employee understands the underlying reasons why the organization has to embark on the planned changes. This insight can gain the employees support as they realise it is in the best interests of the company.

2. The employees will more likely want to join forces with the management to make the changes a success, rather than fighting against them.

3. The employees will be more willing to share their knowledge and insights on how to improve products or services. In addition they might have ideas as to how to improve efficiency and cut costs on the front line.

4. By discussing the changes with the employees, the organisation is better placed to incorporate the employees' desires and needs in to the change. This is likely to result in higher levels of morale.

5. Everyone who plays a part is responsible for the outcome.

Resistance to Change

Consider the concept 'people resist change'. Do you resist change? In answering this question, it can help to recall times in your life when you have experienced change. If you did resist change, what was it about the changes that you resisted? Were there changes that you did not resist? What was it about these changes that made you not resist them?

Reviewing your notes consider whether you agree with the statement 'people resist change.'

Do People Resist Change?

People do not always resist change. It is a mental model that has become ingrained (Dent & Goldberg 1999). A mental model is a collection of thoughts as to how something operates in the world. People are often unaware that they use these mental models and presume that they are in fact reality. Although it is widely believed that people will always resist change, there is actually very little evidence to suggest this is the case.

It could be that the concept of resistance to change has been passed down, as Kuhn (1970) suggests. Dent & Galloway's (1999) support this suggestion. They conducted an analysis of management textbooks. They discovered that the term 'resistance to change' was in the vast majority of textbooks as a given fact, rather than as a concept that needed exploring. In general, people very rarely resist change which results in positive outcomes in their lives. They are far more likely to resist change which will affect their lives in a negative manner. People don't resist change, they resist loses.

Coch and French (1948) conducted a study in a pyjama factory in Virginia. They wanted to investigate why people resist change and how this resistance could be managed. The title of this piece of work was 'Overcoming Resistance to Change' and this is where the term originated from. Their research concluded that when employees were involved in the process, they were less likely to resist the changes.

The study increased the popularity of the concept of 'resistance to change'. It is claimed that the researchers were simply illustrating that it was beneficial to involve employees in the change process. They were not inferring that employees will consistently resist change.

ADKAR

When an organisation is going through a change process, the employees may well support the notion of the new changes and wish to work hard to make the changes successful. However, various obstacles can prevent successful change from occurring.

ADKAR was developed by Prosci in 1998. ADKAR is a tool which enables organisations to analyse how employees are managing the changes and if there are particular aspects they are finding problematic. Once the aspect has been identified, work can begin to overcome the obstacles that the employee is facing. The elements are:

Awareness
Desire
Knowledge
Ability
Reinforcement

Consider an employee who is affected by the change programme. It might be useful to consider a particular individual if you suspect they currently have, or might have in the future, difficulties with change.

Note down your responses to the following:

Awareness of the need to change: To what degree is the individual aware of the reasons for the organisational change (1 - 5 where 1 is no awareness and 5 is total awareness).

Desire to make the change happen: From the individual's perspective, list the possible outcomes that they might be predicting as a result of the change. Consider both the positive and negative outcomes. Analyse the list as a whole and rate his/her desire to change on a 1 - 5 scale.

Knowledge about how to change: Consider to what extent the person truly understands how their working life will differ as a result of the organisational changes. Contemplate the skills and knowledge the individual will require in order for them to adapt to the changes successfully. Rate this person's knowledge or level of training in these areas on a 1 to 5 scale.

Ability to change: Consider if the individual has the ability to utilise the skills and knowledge they hold in order to adapt to the changes successfully. Rate this person's ability to implement the new skills, knowledge and behaviours to support the change on a 1 - 5 scale.

Ability to change: Consider if the individual is able to successfully manage the changes required by drawing on their own resources, skills and knowledge. Rate on a 1 to 5 scale, the extent to which other activities are reinforcing and supporting the change.

Can identify which aspects of the change the individual requires further assistance with? This might be further training or changes in organisational processes to align fully to the change process. An action plan can then be devised.

You might find it useful to use the ADKAR process to analyse three or more other team members. You can then compare your results and assess whether the ADKARs are similar. If some aspects of the ADKAR are similar, it will highlight if there are any particular elements of the change programme that require further evaluation. It can also indicate how your team members are coping differently with the changes taking place in the organisation.

Emotions to Expect During Change Programmes

Recall a time when you have experienced changes within the workplace. Even if there is not a large scale change programme that you have as a reference, many organisations experience various elements of change.

What emotions did you or team experience? What emotions are employees likely to experience during change programmes? For each emotion that you have listed, try to speculate as to why this emotion would occur.

GRASS

Grass illustrates some common emotions that are experienced during a period of change:

Guilt
Resentment
Anxiety
Self Absorption
Stress

Guilt

Managers often experience feelings of guilt as they have had to make people redundant, transfer them to different departments or reduce their responsibilities. Employees can experience guilt too if they have remained in their position yet their colleagues have lost their jobs.

When experiencing feelings of guilt, managers might make an extra effort to display acts of kindness. They might refrain from providing negative feedback even though it is required. Alternatively, some managers may opt to suppress feelings of guilt which could result in an increase of aggressive behaviours.

Resentment

Resentment can build during a change process. Both managers and managed can feel resentment at the upheaval the change has imposed. This is a natural reaction to the losses the individuals are experiencing. These negative emotions can build up and soak into the very core of the organisation if it is not managed sensitively.

Anxiety

Anxiety is another natural reaction as people fear what the future will bring and long for the stability of the past. Feelings of anxiety can result in lower levels of motivation, concentration, performance and creativity. It can also result in higher than usual error and accident rates.

Self-absorption

If people are feeling nervous about the changes, they are more likely to focus inwards, resulting in self-absorption. They lose interest and concern for others which in a work environment can affect team work, customer service and product/service quality.

Stress

Stress is a common emotion experienced during the change process. High levels of stress can result in similar outcomes of both anxiety and self-absorption. It has a high risk of resulting in ill health due to the many diseases that are caused or aggravated by stress.

Stages of Response (Kubler Ross 1973)

There are different stages of response when people experience change. Kubler Ross studied people who were suffering with fatal cancer. She discovered that on hearing the news people would initially be in denial. This was followed by anger, then bargaining, depression and finally acceptance.

Research has shown that people experiencing any type of change, pass through similar stages. As change can often result in experiencing a loss of some kind, they are prone to feelings of grief. In Kubler's research the loss was the loss of life. In relation to the workplace, this loss might relate to reduced working hours or threat of redundancy. The stages that people pass through in an organisational change context are: shock, defensive retreat, acknowledgement and finally adaption and change.

1. Shock

The first reaction is one of shock as they realise their current situation, in which they feel secure, is under threat. This stage tends to evoke feelings of anxiety as they solely focus on potential loses and how this might impact of their lives. This anxiety impacts on their performance, productivity and general well being.

2. Defensive Retreat

In an attempt to stop the change from happening, people attempt to hold on to the old processes and procedures.

3. Acknowledgement

At this stage people start to let go and begin to investigate how they can manage the changes imposed upon them.

4. Adaption & Change

Finally people have adapted to the new situation, together with its new processes and procedures.

The Three Phase Process of Change

Bridges (1991, 2003) suggests there are 3 phases people pass through during organisational change. These three phrases are:

1. Letting Go
2. Neutral Zone - This is the in-between time.
3. New Beginning

Letting Go

In the current situation, before the change, the individual feels secure. They are confident and comfortable as they have all the knowledge and skills to complete the job successfully. Any future plans for progression or personal development are based on the current state.

It is vitally important at this stage to identify and prepare for the losses the individual will experience as a result of the change. Failure to do so can greatly hinder the success of an organisational change programme.

Identifying losses

Sometimes these losses are not obvious at first glance. Managers need to be careful not to put their own judgements on to the losses of others and deem them unimportant. It is important that managers are very clear about what will and will not change. This clears up any confusion and reduces the risk of rumours spreading. It is important to acknowledge the losses that individuals will experience and show empathy.

Write a list of what your team members might lose as a result of the planned changes.

What are individuals losing? Is everyone losing the same things or are people losing different things? What is the team losing?

Acknowledge the Past

Speak of the past in a positive light. Keep in mind that many people will think fondly of the past and will fiercely defend it if it is attacked. This defense will further increase resistance to change.

Ensure that people do not have to let go of everything old. It might mean a bit of creativity is needed in order to allow something old to remain.

Acknowledge how the previous way of working brought success to the business. Reconfirm the reasons behind the need for the change and emphasise any similarities between the past, present and future.

Acknowledge emotions

- Ensure you fully listen to people's perspectives on what they are losing. Don't dismiss their perspective. Disagreeing with the way they see things will create tension and is unlikely to change their mind at this stage

Expect over reactions, expect anger.

Expect anxiety. Consider if some individuals might be concerned that they are not capable of carrying out the tasks that will be required. Is there the possibility that training, mentoring or coaching could bridge any skills gaps?

Change cause losses. It is these losses that the people are reacting to, not the changes. Ignoring the existence of such losses can cause problems.

Try to achieve the following actions

Provide information in a variety of formats such as letters, memos, newsletters, intranet, meetings and presentations. Do not presume that because the employees were informed by one letter that every individual has memorised all the key points. It is important to reinforce the message.

Remember to reiterate the reasons the organization is making these changes. If possible let them experience it first-hand. For example, if the change is as a result of customer complaints, show them the customer complaint data. Ensure they appreciate the changes are urgent.

Consider if there is anything that could be given to compensate for the losses experienced. This could be status, recognition, mentoring, training etc.

The initial changes that take place might cause secondary changes. These can be less obvious to the managers, yet matter a great deal to the individuals. If an employee appears to be resisting the changes, it may be that a secondary change is the cause.

As an example of a secondary change consider an individual who currently enjoys long lunch breaks. They presently work in a room separate to their manager so nobody takes note of when they leave or return from lunch. They have been using this to their full advantage and have been taking at least 1 ½ hours for lunch every day. The changes will require them to move into the office with their manager. This in turn will require them to take lunch in the allotted time. This individual might be creating a lot of resistance about moving office, yet the management can't understand why. In this situation the management would continue as planned and the individual will eventually adapt to the new way of working. Other secondary changes can be changed to make the individual more comfortable with the changes.

Consider what secondary changes could exist within your work place. Make an exhaustive list.

Neutral Zone

Next is the neutral zone. This is the in-between phase, where the old methods of working are no longer appropriate and the new methods are not fully functional.

Kotter (1995) studied over 100 organisations experiencing organisational change. Kotter reported that often employees supported the changes and wished to help the organisation make the changes a success, however they were facing various obstacles which were impacting on their ability to make the required changes.

Various aspects of the role might not be aligned with the new vision. In order to understand any obstacles that the employees are facing, managers can ask what is helping and what is hindering the change efforts. In doing so, other departments can learn from their experiences and obstacles can be managed more effectively. By doing so employees are more likely to feel committed to the change goals, feel part of a team and take responsibility for the changes required (Carnall 1990).

Managers should enquire about obstacles regularly. As the individual moves through the change process they can discover obstacles that were not apparent at the beginning.

There is a great deal of psychological change during the neutral zone as viewpoints are altered and the past starts to give way to the future.

What problems do you envisage employees experiencing in the neutral zone? What emotions might employees experience? What impact could this have on the work?

Dangers of the Neutral Zone

There are many dangers of the neutral zone:

- High anxiety levels
- Low motivation
- Emotions run high – employees often over-analyse or make negative predictions
- Sick days increase as employees struggle to manage this unsettling period
- Weaknesses previously hidden are suddenly exposed

On a positive note, it is also a very creative time. At times employees and managers can get stuck in old patterns of working that are largely ineffective. One great benefit of the neutral zone is the freedom to improve processes and procedures.

Leading People through the Neutral Zone

When thinking about change people usually expect to move from the old to the new instantly. They fail to realise that there will be a period of uncertainty in between. One of the manager's roles during a change programme is to educate their team members that a neutral zone exists. This awareness will help their employees accept the uncertainty during this period.

Discussions regarding the neutral zone may include how to manage obstacles that have not been foreseen. It can also be useful to discuss expected emotions during this period. Plans can be developed in order to manage this often confusing period. These plans could include temporary systems.

If employees have a clear vision of how the period of the neutral zone is enabling them to move towards the overall change goals, they are more likely to manage the change effectively. employees are unable to see how a change contributes to the achievement of the overall vision, it can cause distress. Unexpected changes can also unsettle them.

The neutral zone is a period of turbulence. Whilst some people can enjoy the freedom of this period, others will find it deeply unsettling. It can be very tempting to rush through it as quickly as possible in order to regain stability. This might involve pushing for quick decisions rather than spending time investigating the best solutions for the organisation.

Throughout the neutral zone it is important that managers clearly communicate with their team. It helps to reduce risk and ambiguity (Pugh 1993). A lack of communication can result in people trying to mind-read managers or predict the future. This can result in negative rumours spreading through the organisation raising anxiety levels even further. The repeated use of memo's, meetings, newsletters and presentations can help to clearly communicate and reinforce the plans.

Goals from personal appraisals or reward schemes will need to be reviewed in order to ensure they align to the neutral zone. Previous goals, rewards, policies, procedures and even roles may reinforce the old methods. Temporary goals and systems are sometimes required to enable a smooth transition through the neutral zone, before being changed again for the New Beginning.

The setting of short term goals can be used to guide people through the neutral zone and create a sense of achievement. This can provide an additional motivating benefit as the employees can see the changes are starting to work.

Managing Conflict In the Neutral Zone

During the neutral zone, the heightened negative emotions can result in more conflicts occurring. This might relate to people feeling insecure, anxious or under threat. They might also still be grieving about the losses they have incurred. When in a conflict situation allow the individual to inform you of their concerns, do not interrupt. This information can be a great insight into how others are also feeling, yet are reluctant to share with you. Listen intently and assess whether you can fix any of the points raised. Showing this commitment to listening and actively trying to improve things for the individual, will help to keep communication channels open in the future.

New Beginning

The New Beginning stage marks the fact that the changes are operational and new working practices have been incorporated into the workplace. People discover the new way of working and experience the new energy it creates. This can be an exciting time yet it is not without its dangers. Certain anxieties can reside around the new beginning. People may remember the past, when they tried something new and failed. If this is the case managers can remind them of the problems that existed and why the change was needed in the first place. They can create a vision of the future and reinforce the benefits these changes will bring. Providing support and adequate training, to ensure employees have the capability to carry out the new tasks required of them, is essential.

Individuals might be concerned that the future state does not match their personal development plans. For example, an employee may have been undertaking formal training which now appears less relevant to their new role or they may realise that their chances of promotion have decreased due to fewer higher level roles. If this is the case consider what you can replace this 'loss' with. Perhaps you can offer coaching and mentoring to further their development, might there be alternative promotion opportunities in the future, would the person like to take on more managerial responsibilities to gain skills and experience, is there a training course they would like to pursue, etc?

Why Transformation Efforts Fail

Studies have been conducted on organisational change for decades. Kotter (1995) has identified 8 common errors that decrease the effectiveness and success of change programmes.

Error 1: Failure to create a sense of urgency.

If employees feel that there is no urgency to the change, a feeling of malaise can occur which can de-motivate and slow down the change process. This in turn can lead to an overall unsuccessful outcome. Urgency can be created through the use of customer data, financial data and reviews of the competition.

Error 2: Not creating a powerful enough group of guiding leaders.

You need to have an influential group of people to manage the change process. Usually it is best to involve line managers as they have influence within their own teams and can provide insight into how the separate sections of the organisation operate as a whole. The group can be fairly small for example 3-5 people, or considerably larger for large organisations.

Error 3: Lacking a vision.

The change management team need to create a simple vision for the future. If it is too complicated people will not be able to comprehend its many parts and will tend to simplify the version in their own minds. This can lead to misunderstandings and confusion when the change programme is undertaken. Ideally you will be able to communicate the **overall** vision and the subsequent plans in under 5 minutes.

Additional time will be required when explaining the finer details relevant to each department.

Error 4: Under-communicating the vision by a factor of ten.

On some occasions change plans are communicated in one single meeting. This is not enough for employees to fully digest the vision and subsequent plans. It needs to be reinforced continually. This can be achieved by managers acting as role models and continually demonstrating the new working practices.

Error 5: Not removing obstacles to the new vision.

Sometimes obstacles can make people choose between working towards the new vision or serving their own self-interest. This can occur if a reward system does not get realigned to the new way of working. The employee then faces the dilemma of working the new way and not receiving rewards, or working the old way and receiving their rewards.

Managers might not be fully engaged in the new initiatives and instead just pay them lip service. This can keep the old methods of working alive, damaging the likelihood of successful outcomes from the change efforts.

Error 6: Not systematically creating short term wins.

Create short term goals so people can experience short term wins. Sometimes change programmes can take years from start to finish. If people do not experience a sense of achievement and a feeling of progression, momentum can falter. Ensuring they experience short term wins can keep them motivated and encourage them to maintain a sense of urgency.

Error 7: Declaring victory too soon.

Initial results could indicate that it appears that the change has been successful but it is important that these initial results are not blown out of proportion. Whilst managers should celebrate this achievement, the need for continuing the change needs to be communicated. It can take 5 to 10 years before the changes soak into the core of the organisation. If success is declared too early, the change efforts can start to fade. Traditional ways of working seep back in and the organisation starts to slip back to the previous state.

Error 8: Not anchoring changes in the organisations culture.

It is vital that managers continually reinforce the changes by acting as a role model and encouraging their team members to work with the new practices. It is important they regularly remind employees of the current and future impact of the changes.

Appreciative Inquiry Method for Change Programmes

Activity

Consider that your organisation wishes to embark upon a change programme. The aim of the change programme might be to increase efficiency or profits. For the purpose of this activity, choose one primary aim.

Consider the process of how you would design the change process. Think about:

Who would be involved?
How would the aims, objectives and goals be decided upon?
Would it look to 'fix' problems within company? If so, how would you know what to fix?
Would input from the employees inform the change programme? Keep these answers in mind as you will be asked to refer to them later on.

What is Appreciative Inquiry?

Appreciative Inquiry (A.I.) was developed by Cooperrider and Srivastva (1987). A.I. is a positive focused method used in change programmes. It is considered to be both a philosophy and a methodology. Many companies are now using Appreciative Inquiry to release the potential in their business and the potential in their employees. A.I. can be used on large scale change programmes across organisations or smaller group based projects. A.I. is often more effective than traditional change efforts.

Appreciative Inquiry uses a strength based approach. It is different to traditional problem solving approaches. Appreciative Inquiry reflects on what people value. It creates an organisation around what the members want it to be. It is based on the notion that an organisation will develop in the direction of what it focuses upon. This focus infiltrates how the questions are phrased to itself and its employees (Cooperrider 1990).

The method works on the premise that it is just as important to reflect on the future, as it is to reflect on the past. Reflecting on the future is termed 'Anticipatory Reality'. When individuals are able to speak about what really matters to them, real change is more likely to occur.

Employee Engagement

The Appreciative Inquiry method aims to involve all relevant employees, even if this means involving the whole organisation or group. Every individual is involved from the very beginning. The employees are involved in the whole process from defining to designing to implementing the change. They are therefore also responsible for the outcome and will naturally show higher levels of commitment.

As everybody is involved in the Appreciative Inquiry process, information is disseminated to each and every individual. There is a shared understanding of how the end vision was created. This helps to create open channels of communication throughout the organisation.

A.I. provides individuals with the ability to understand how they fit into the overall strategy. Whilst everyone is working towards their own personal goals, they can see how their personal goals fit into their team and their organisations' overall success. If you compare this to a traditional change programme sometimes this can be difficult and a feeling of separation can occur.

AI encourages the employees of an organisation to work together as a whole in order to achieve the overall aims. This naturally creates a positive work environment which leads to increased performance, productivity, creativity and morale.

The Positive Principle

Organisations need to encourage employees to focus on their positive core. This includes an appraisal of their strengths, successes and visions for the future. Discussions around the ideal future can be a great catalyst for organisational change (Ludema 2001).

If problems are used to drive a change effort, the organisation can find itself with an over whelming number of problems to solve. If a positive focus is used to drive a change effort and creativity is encouraged, this can lead to far greater successful outcomes. Words create worlds (Whitney 1998).

The goal is to build upon the organisations' positive core and incorporate this in to creating a desired vision and plan for the future. This positive approach builds motivation and a desire for change. As a result, appreciative inquiry change efforts often lead to measurable, sustainable results.

Look back over your notes for the Activity earlier in this section. Is it a deficit based approach? Does it look at aspects of the company that are not working and how these could be improved?

If so, spend time considering why the approach you chose is problem focused. Is it the most natural way to initiate change? Is it the way that you engage with change on a personal level? Is it how your organisation currently tries to evoke change? Does change only occur when there are problems to be fixed?

Many people find that when they are looking to make changes they naturally use a problem focused approach. They look at what is wrong and what is not working. Their plans are around how to fix the problem.

Appreciative Inquiry looks at what is working within an organisation and builds upon this. This helps to encourage positive change. It does not focus on problems. What are your initial thoughts on this?

Appreciative Inquiry Critics

When people first hear about Appreciative Inquiry, one of the first criticisms is that 'Sometimes problems have to be fixed. Ignoring them and focusing on the positive isn't going to fix them'.

Appreciative Inquiry can be used to solve identified problems For example, let's say a company's profits are generally down. The solution is to look at how to improve profits. Appreciative Inquiry would look at what parts of the business are most profitable, what is working well in these areas and whether it is possible to apply this to other areas or business products.

Another comment we often hear is, 'If something is NOT working in the organisation then surely we need to identify this? It could be that we focus on solutions and the positive core, but this one thing stops the organisation from moving forward?'

It might be that by focusing on what is working well naturally eradicates what is not working so well. Alternatively if it makes you more comfortable you can first look at problems then re-frame these positively into points of action.

5D Appreciative Inquiry Model

Here is the 5D Appreciative Inquiry Model:

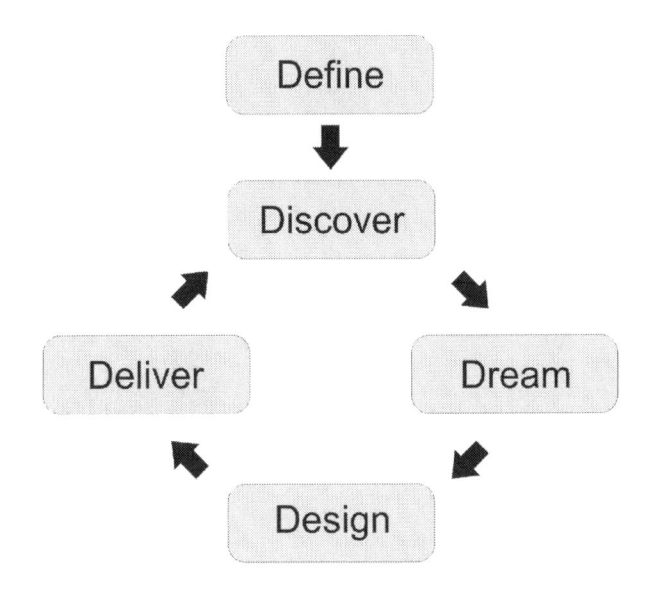

```
        Define
           ↓
        Discover
       ↗        ↘
  Deliver        Dream
       ↖        ↙
        Design
```

Define

The Define stage looks at identifying aspects to be changed. These aspects might be problems that exist within the organisation or growth opportunities that need exploring.

If the aspect is problem based such as 'poor customer satisfaction', re-frame this to a positive goal such as, 'improving customer satisfaction levels'. Re-framing problems this way is more likely to motivate and encourage commitment from employees.

Discover Phase

The discover phase focuses on:

- Identifying strengths and successes.
- Exploring the highpoints of success.

In the discover phase we collect stories from employees of when the organisation was performing at its most excellent (Bushe 1999):

Let's imagine that a company wishes to improve customer loyalty. The Appreciative Inquiry process would ask employees to share their stories of when customers have remained loyal. This might be individual incidents or it might relate to a period in the past. If the organisation was looking to improve performance levels, stories would be collected relating to when performance levels were high.

This phase also looks at:

- Creating a vision of what success looks like
- Identifying which aspects are of the most personal or material value

Dream Phase

Next is the dream phase. This phase involves:

- Envisioning what could happen.
- Envisioning outcomes.
- Envisioning impacts of these outcomes.

This phase incorporates the elements of the define and discovery phases to develop a shared vision of the dream future. The dream future will ideally detail as much as possible to ensure that people can envisage it fully. The detail also ensures that all those involved in the process are envisioning the same future.

Design Phase

The outputs from the previous define, discover and dream phase are used to inform the design phase. This phase works to plan how the future vision can be achieved. The planning can involve designing roles, structures, initiatives, reward schemes, procedures, processes, policies and mission statements.

Deliver Phase

The deliver phase involves putting the plans from the design phase into action. Change is encouraged, taking care to maintain the positive core. Employees might face challenges in this phase of the process as they adapt to the new working methods.

Appreciative Inquiry in Practice

Ideally the Appreciative Inquiry process would involve the whole organisation Some organisations will take a complete week to complete the define, discover and design stages. This is then followed up with sessions in the weeks and months that follow. Some organisations hire consultants to carry out the process whilst others opt for doing it themselves.

We are now going to look at how to carry out the actual process.

Define Phase

Define your aims for the organisation.

Depending on the situation, you may wish to define your aims with the senior management team and involve the whole organisation at the later discovery phase.

Your objectives might look something like this..........

> Your Logo
>
> <u>Objectives - Appreciative Inquiry Session on Date Here</u>
>
> 1. To achieve higher customer satisfaction scores.
> 2. To provide the best service delivery possible.
> 3. To reinforce our company ethos.
> 4.
> 5.
> 6.

Discover Phase

In the discover phase it is easier to initially work in small groups and then feed back to the larger group.

In addition to this, it is often best for people to take some time to think through their own thoughts before they share them with their small group. This helps the individuals to collect their thoughts with ease. It also helps to ensure that everyone's thoughts are heard.

Below is an example of a handout you could design for the Discover Phase.

>   Your Logo
>
> ### Appreciative Inquiry
> ### Discovery Phase
>
> Talk with your group to discover when our organisation was functioning at its best. When telling these stories use as much detail as possible. This will help us to discover the 'positive core' of our organisation.
>
> 1. Think of a high point in your working life at this company

Your Logo

2. In that experience what helped you to succeed in relation to:

a) Your strengths

b) The role and nature of the work

c) The organisation

3. What gives 'life' to our organisation. What positive values and beliefs should we build on?

Other questions you might ask in the Discover Phase:
What works well?
What has worked well in the past?
Even if something is not working at the moment, are there aspects of it that are working?

After an Appreciative Inquiry meeting, it can be beneficial to collate the information from the discovery phase and present it to the employees. It could be presented as a document or as a wall display within the workplace. This is used to celebrate and remind all the employees of the strengths of the employees and the company.

Dream Phase

Once the discovery phase has been shared with everyone, it is time to think about the dream phase. This phase involves creating a detailed vision of what an ideal future would look like for the organisation. This is best done in small groups and then fed back to the larger group to collate a 'shared' dream.

Below is an example of a handout you might create for the Dream Phase.

> Your Logo
>
> ## Appreciative Inquiry Dream Phase
>
> Discuss in your small groups your dreams for the organisation. Refer back to the objectives. You might like to consider:
>
> - What would be an ideal future for the organisation?
> - What are the possibilities?
> - What would the successful outcomes look like? What would be happening?
> - What impact would these successful outcomes have?

Design Phase

Next is the Design Phase. Ideally the large group needs to work together on designing a practical and achievable plan to achieve the dream. You might want to consider:

- Roles
- Structures
- Policies, procedures, processes

- Initiatives
- Training, coaching, mentoring
- Timescales

Deliver Phase

This is the actual doing part. It involves putting into place the action plan that was built around the positive core. Regular meetings and reviews would be beneficial in order to check progress and continue to move things forward.

Future Progressions

As time progresses it might be appropriate to re-visit the discover phase and start the cycle again.

On your own, complete a mini mock run through of the appreciative inquiry process. This activity will act as a revision of the concepts, so do look back through the book in order to inform your plan. Your Appreciative Inquiry Plan would include:

- A list of possible organisation objectives.
- A list of possible questions you would use in the discover and dream phase.
- A mock completion of these questions from your personal perspective.
- A list of the areas you would then need to consider in the design process.
- A mock action plan which includes time scales for action points and follow up meetings.

References

Argyris, C. (1994). On Organisational Learning. Oxford: Blackwell.

Arnold, J. (2005). Work Psychology. Understanding Human Behaviour in the Workplace. Prentice Hall.

Audia, P.G. and Locke. E.A. (2003). Benefiting from Negative Feedback. Human Resources Management Review, Vol. 13, Issue 4, pp. 631-646.

Belbin, R.M. (1993). Team Roles at Work: A Strategy for Human Resource Management. Oxford: Butterworth-Heinemann.

Bridges, W. (1991) Managing Transitions

Bridges, W. (2003) Making the Most of Change.

Bushe, G. (1999). Five theories of change embedded in appreciative inquiry. In Appreciative Inquiry: Rethinking human organization toward a positive theory of change.

Carnall, C.A, (1990) Managing Change in Organizations, London: Prentice Hall

Cartwright, S. and Cooper, C.L. (1997). Managing Workplace Stress. London: Sage.

Coch,L., French, J.R.P., Jr (1948) Overcoming Resistance to Change. Human Relations, I (4), 512-532.

Connell, B and Palmer, S. (2007) Solution-focused Coaching. Handbook of Coaching Psychology.

Conner-Smith, J.K. and Flachsbart, C. (2007). Relations Between Personality and Coping: A Meta-Analysis. Journal of Personality and Social Psychology, vol 93, issue 6, p. 1080-1107

Cooper, C. (1996). Working Hours and Health. Work and Stress, Vol.10(1), pp.1-4.

Cooper, C.L., Sloan, S. and Williams, S. (1988b). Occupational Stress Indicator: The Manual Windsor. NFER-Nelson.

Cooperrider, D.L (1990). Positive Image, Positive Action: The Affirmative Basis of Organising.

Cooperrider, D. L., & Srivastva, S. (1998). An Invitation to Organizational Wisdom and Executive Courage. In S. Srivastva & D. L. Cooperrider (Eds.)

Cox, T. (1980) Repetitive Work. Cooper, C.L. and Payne, R. (eds) Current Concerns in Occupational Stress. Chichester: John Wiley.

Cummings, T. and Cooper, C. (1979). A Cybernetic Framework for the Study of Occupational Stress. Human Relations, Vol.32, pp.395-419.

Dawson, P. (1994) Organisational Change: A Processual Approach. London: Paul Chapman Publishing

Dent, E.B., Goldberg, S.G. (1999). Challenging "Resistance to Change". Journal of Applied Behavioural Science, 35;21.

Druskat, V. U., & Wolff, S. B. (2001). Group Emotional Competence and its Influence on Group effectiveness. In Cary Cherniss and Daniel Goleman (Eds.), Goleman, D. (1999). Working with Emotional Intelligence. Bloomsbury Publishing.

D'Zurilla, T.J. and Goldfried, M.R. (1971). Problem Solving and Behaviour Modification. Journal of Abnormal Psychology. Vol.78, Issue 1, pp. 107-126.

Eichinger, R.W. and Lombardo, M. M. (2004). The 6 Qs of Management: A Blueprint for Enduring Success at the Top. Lominger, The Management Architects.

Finkelstein, S. (2003). Why Smart Executive Fail: And What You Can Learn From Their Mistakes. Portfolio.

Fitzpatrick, M.R. and Stalikas, A. (2008). Positive Emotions as Generators of Change. Journal of Psychotherapy Integration, Vol. 18, Issue 2, pp.137-154.

Francis, D. (1994). Managing Your Own Career. Harper Collins.

Grant, A.M. and Palmer, S. (2002).Coaching Psychology Workshop. Annual Conference of the Division of Counselling Psychology, British Psychological Society, Torquay UK, 18th May.

Greene, J and Grant, A.M. (2003). Solution Focused Coaching. Harlow, UK: Pearson Education.

Hersey, P. and Blanchard, K. H. (1969). Life Cycle Theory of Management. Training and Development Journal, Vol, 23, Issue 5, 26–34.

Ivancevich, J.M. and Matteson, M.T, (1980). Stress and Work. Glenview, H, Scott, Foresman and Co.

Janis, I, L. (1972). Groupthink. Boston. MA: Houghton Mifflin.

Jia-Sheng Heh (1999). Evaluation Model of Problem Solving. Mathematical and Computer Modelling. Vol. 30, Issues 11-12, pp.197-211.

Kerr,N.L and Bruun, S.E. (1983) Dispensability of Member Effort and Group Motivation Losses: Free-rider Effects. Journal of Personality and Social Psychology, Vol. 44, pp.78-94.

Kilburg, R.R. (1996). Toward a Conceptual Understanding and Definition of Executive Coaching. Consulting Psychology Journal: Practice and Research 48, pp. 134-144.

Kilburg, R. R, (1997). Coaching and Executive Character: Core Problems and Basic Approaches. Consulting Psychology Journal: Practice and Research 53, pp. 251-267.

Kombarakaran, F.A., Yang, J.A., Baker, M.N. and Fernandes, P.B. (2008). Executive Coaching: It Works! Consulting Psychology Journal: Practice and Research. Vol.60, Issue 1, pp.78-90.

Kotter,J.P. (1995) Leading Change. Why Transformation Efforts Fail.

Kraft, R.G., Claiborn, C.D. and Dowd, E.T. (1985). Effectiveness Effects of Positive Reframing and Paradoxical Directives in Counseling for Negative Emotions. Journal of Counselling Psychology. Vol 32, Issue 4, pp. 617-621.

Kübler-Ross, E. (1973) On Death and Dying, Routledge.

Kuhn,T.S. (1970) The Structure of Scientific Revolutions (2nd ed). Chicago: University of Chicago Press

Latane, B., Williams, K. and Harkins, S. (1979) Many Hands Make Light Work: The Causes and Consequences of Social Loafing. Journal of Personality and Social Psychology, Vol. 37, pp.822-832.

Lazarus,r.S. (1966) Psychological Stress & Coping Process. New York: McGraw-Hill.

Levenson, A. (2009). Measuring and Maximizing The Business Impact of Executive Coaching. Consulting Psychology Journal, Vol.61, Issue 2, pp. 103-121.

Lizzio, A., Wilson, K., & MacKay, L. (2008). Managers' and Subordinates' Evaluations of Feedback Strategies: The Critical Contribution of Voice. Journal of Applied Social Psychology, , 38 (4), 919–946.

Locke, E.A. and Latham, G. P. (1990). A Theory of Goal Setting and Task Performance. Englewood Cliffs, NJ, Prentice Hall.

Ludema, J.(2001). From Deficit Discourse to Vocabularies of Hope: The Power of Appreciation. Appreciative Inquiry: An Emerging Direction for Organisation Development (first ed)

Malouff, J.M., Thorsteinsson, E.B. and Schutte, N.S. (2007). The Efficacy of Problem Solving Therapy in Reducing Mental and Physical Health Problems: A Meta-analysis. Clinical Psychology Review, Vol. 27, Issue 1, pp. 46-57.

Marrow, A.J. (1977) The Practical Theorist: The Life and Work of Kurt Lewin. New York: Teachers College Press.

Meindl, J.R., Ehrlich, S.B. and Dukerich, J.M. (1985). The Romance of Management. Administrative Science Quarterly, Vol. 30, pp. 78-102.

Myers, Isabel Briggs; Mary H. McCaulley (1985). Manual: A Guide to the Development and Use of the Myers-Briggs Type Indicator (2nd ed.). Palo Alto, CA: Consulting Psychologists Press.

Nonaka, I. (1988) Creating Organizational Order out of Chaos: Self Renewal in Japenese Firms' Harvard Business Review, November/December, pp. 96-104.

Pavlov, I.P. (1927/1960). Conditional Reflexes. New York: Dover Publications (the 1960 edition is an unaltered republication of the 1927 translation by Oxford University Press).

Pritchard, R.D., Campbell, K.M. and Campbell, D.J. (1976). Effects of Extrinsic Financial Rewards on Intrinsic Motivation. Journal of Applied Psychology, Vol. 62, Issue 1, pp. 9-15.

Pugh, D. (1993) Understanding and Managing Organisational Change. Mabey, C. and Mayon-White, B (eds) Managing Change, 2nd Edition. London: Open University/Paul Chapman Publishing.

Rosenman,R.H., Friedman,M. and Straus,R. (1964) A predictive Study of CHD. Journal of the Medical Association, vol.189, pp.15-22.

Selye, H. (1975). "Confusion and Controversy in the Stress Field". *Journal of Human Stress* **1**: 37–44.

Seo, M. & Remus, I. (2009). The Role of Self-efficacy, Goal, and Affect in Dynamic Motivational Self-regulation. Organizational Behavior and Human Decision Processes, 109, 120–133.

Skinner, B. F. (1974). About Behaviorism. New York: Knopf.

Snyder, C.R. and Cowles, C. (1979). Impact of Positive and Negative Feedback Based on Personality and Intellectual Assessment. Journal of Consulting and Clinical Psychology, Volume 47, Issue 1, pp. 207-209.

Sosik,J.J. and Godshalk,V.M. (2000) Leadership Styles, Mentoring Functions Received, and Job-Related Stress: A Conceptual Model and Preliminary Study. Journal of Organizational Behaviour, vol 21, pp.365-90.

Sutherland, V, and Cooper, C.L. (2000). Strategic Stress Management. London. Macmillan.

Tucker, P. and Knowles, S.R. (2008).Review of Studies that have used the Standard Shiftwork Index: Evidence for the Underlying Shiftwork and Health. Applied Ergonomics, vol 39, issue 5, 550-564.

Tucker, P. and Rutherford, C (2005). Moderators of the Relationship Between Long Work Hours and Health. Journal of Occupational Health Psychology. Vol 10, Issue 4, p.465-475

Wasylyshyn, K.M., Gronsky, B., Independent Consultant, Haas, W.J. (2006). Tigers, Stripes and Behaviour Change: Survey Results of a Commissioned Coaching Program. Consulting

Watkins, J.M., Cooperrider,D.L.(2000). Appreciative Inquiry: A transformative paradigm. Journal of the Organization Development Network. Vol.32. 6-12.

Whitney,D. (1998). Let's Change the Subject and Change our Organization: an Appreciative Inquiry Approach to Organization Change.

Wood, A.M., Linley, A., Maltby, J., Kashdan, D.B., Hurling, R. (2011). Using Personal and Psychological Strengths Leads to Increases in Well-being

Over Time: A Longitudinal Study and the Development of the Strengths Use Questionnaire. Personality and Individual Differences. Vol. 50, Issue 1, pp.15-19.

Zenger, J. and Folkman, J. (2009). Ten Fatal Flaws that Derail Managers. Harvard Business Review.

More books by this author

Presentation Skills: Portraying Confidence, Answering Tricky Questions and Structuring Content

What Other Marketing Books Won't Tell You: A Brutally Honest Account of Marketing a Small Business

The Counselling Sessions: Overcoming Feelings of Irritability and Anger in Relationships

The Counselling Sessions: Overcoming Anxiety and Panic Attacks

The Counselling Sessions: Overcoming Low Mood and Depression

Printed in Great Britain
by Amazon